About *The Believer* magazine

The Believer is a magazine offering essays, interviews, reviews, and advice, the latter of which appears in the form of a monthly column called "Sedaratives." The Sedaratives column, which started in May 2005 with advice by Amy Sedaris, gave rise to this book.

About the Editors

Mike Sacks is on the editorial staff of *Vanity Fair* magazine. His work has appeared in *Vanity Fair, The New Yorker, Esquire, GQ, Salon, The New York Times, The Washington Post, McSweeney's, The Believer, Vice,* and other publications. Sacks is the author of three books: *And Here's the Kicker: Conversations with 21 Top Humor Writers on Their Craft; SEX: Our Bodies, Our Junk;* and *Your Wildest Dreams, Within Reason.*

Eric Spitznagel is a contributing editor for *The Believer* magazine, where he cocreated (along with Amy Sedaris) the Sedaratives column. He's also the author of six books and a frequent contributor to *Playboy* and *Vanity Fair.* He has one more testicle than Hitler, which he considers a moral victory.

Also by *The Believer*

You're a Horrible Person, But I Like You:
The Believer Book of Advice

Care to Make Love in That Gross Little Space Between Cars?

A **BELIEVER** BOOK OF ADVICE

Care to Make Love in That Gross Little Space Between Cars?

A **BELIEVER** BOOK OF ADVICE

With Louis C.K., Amy Sedaris,
Zach Galifianakis, Nick Hornby, Weird Al &
many more

INTRODUCTION BY JUDD APATOW
A SECOND ATTEMPT AT AN INTRODUCTION
BY PATTON OSWALT

Edited by Mike Sacks and Eric Spitznagel

VINTAGE BOOKS

A Division of Random House, Inc.

New York

A VINTAGE BOOKS ORIGINAL, MARCH 2012

Copyright © 2012 by Believer Inc.

All rights reserved. Published in the United States by Vintage Books,
a division of Random House, Inc., New York, and in Canada by
Random House of Canada Limited, Toronto.

Vintage and colophon are registered trademarks of Random House, Inc.

Many of these selections were first published in *The Believer.*
All selections are copyright to the contributors.

Library of Congress Cataloging-in-Publication Data
Care to make love in that gross little space between cars? : a Believer book of advice /
with Louis C.K., Amy Sedaris, Zach Galifianakis, Nick Hornby, Weird Al & many
more ; introductions by Judd Apatow and Patton Oswalt ; edited by Mike Sacks and
Eric Spitznagel.
   p. cm.
ISBN 978-0-307-74371-8 (pbk.)
   1. American wit and humor.   2. Advice columns—Humor.   I. Sacks, Mike.
II. Spitznagel, Eric.   III. The Believer magazine.
PN6165.C357 2012
814'.54—dc23
2011045561

www.vintagebooks.com

Printed in the United States of America
10 9 8 7 6 5 4 3 2 1

Contents

Care to Make Love in That Gross Little Space Between Cars?

A **BELIEVER** BOOK OF ADVICE

Introduction

Dear Judd Apatow:
We're thinking about publishing a sequel to You're a Horrible Person, But I Like You. *It'd be more or less the same thing as the first book, except with mostly different people, and different questions. Are we being redundant?*

Thanks,
The Believer *magazine*
San Francisco, CA

Dear *The Believer:*
I really don't know how to answer that question. There is a larger issue, which is: Why am I writing the intro to this book at all?

This is a mistake I keep making, saying yes to things for no apparent reason. I don't know if it is because I get insecure or I need an ego stroke, but I keep finding myself in the same position, stuck with something I don't want to do but said yes to because someone did a good job kissing my ass.

I don't even understand what you want. Am I supposed to write something logical, or absurd? I have no idea.

I don't even know if this book is for charity or if someone is going to make a shitload of money off it. I kind of always assumed it benefited some charity, but I don't think that is correct. I also have the vague notion that the entire publishing empire that's releasing it is a nonprofit, but I have no proof and am probably wrong about that. Or I am right.

One thing I do know is I get paid very well for my time and money and I am getting paid zero dollars to write this and that makes no sense at all.

I can't even remember who asked me to do it. Probably someone who seemed smart and who made me feel like less of a dick-joke-writing idiot by asking, and I got all excited for all of five minutes till I realized it actually required real work.

I wouldn't be writing this at all if Paul Rudd wasn't ten minutes late to our meeting. If he'd been on time, today would have been the day I worked up the nerve to bail on this assignment so they could go manipulate some other insecure Jewish man into doing it.

Why not ask a non-Jew? Why not ask a woman? An African American? Someone from South America? Aren't people ready for some new flavors of comedy at this point?

I know I am. I might move to Nicaragua for a year or two just to come up with a new comedic angle that's not based on my Jewish mother's influence and child rearing. Maybe if I started a junta I could write a fresh joke. What is a junta? I need to find out.

Where the hell is Paul Rudd? He is always late. He was never late when his career wasn't going well, but ever since *I Love You, Man* he could give a fuck about wasting my time.

Oh, there he is. Hey, Paul! You look good. I like the beard.

Judd

A Second Attempt at an Introduction

Dear Patton:

So listen, we're doing this book of advice and we asked Judd Apatow to write the intro, and it didn't really work out. We don't want to get into it, but it has something to do with Paul Rudd's career going well. Anyway, is there a chance you might like to take a crack at it? The introduction, we mean.

Thanks in advance,
The Believer *magazine*
San Francisco, CA

Dear *The Believer* magazine:
Wait, so Judd "Heavyweights" Apatow is too busy to finish his introduction and so you figured, "Oh, let's get Patton 'Basic Cable Day Player' Oswalt to pick up the slack"? I

will bet money you used that exact phrase because I really like losing money.

I mean, how busy can I possibly be, right?

"Quite" to "nearly 'very,'" as it turns out! So I hope your readers appreciate the projects I've back-burnered so that there can be a full introduction to this book. And as you read this book, think for a moment about the:

Unalphabetized Travis McGee books on my shelf

Overflowing trash can in my kitchen

Unwatched (and thus undeleted) episodes of *Justified* on my DVR

Not uneaten Rye Krisps, consumed due to the stress of having to write this

Now I will end this introduction early to make it further appear I am busy, just like Judd.

See? I'm making it in Hollywood!

Patton

Kristen Schaal

Dear Kristen:
Are lighthouses still used for what they were meant for or are they just the nation's decorative knickknacks on our coastlines?
                    Cameren Cousins
                    Herndon, VA

Dear Cameren:
I wish they were as useless as giant beautiful plastic flamingos covered in reflector tape. But unfortunately, their importance has magnified in these modern times. Apart from warning boats, canoes, and cross-ocean swimmers of impending land, they serve another function: bringing whale crime to light. Whales have taken their cue from the Somali pirates and have begun to rapidly create havoc in our peaceful seas. Stealing from ghost pirate ships, tagging

reefs, and, more recently, abducting dolphin babies and selling them to infertile manatees. They do their dirty work at night and the lighthouses have been working overtime, combing the waters with their revealing beams after the alarm has been sounded by whatever sea creature can make the walk on land. Usually tattletale crabs.

Kristen

. . .

Dear Kristen:
There's been a lot of hullabaloo about child concussions lately.
Are children more violent these days or were we just overlooked as
children? The shake-off philosophy worked for us, so why can't it
work for modern-day children?

Nick Pappas
Hazelton, PA

Dear Nick:
Or perhaps are children more sleepy these days? Maybe they are using their concussions as excuses to take time-outs from working in the fields or sewing in the sweatshops. Check their tiny hands on their unconscious bodies. If their fingers are worked and bloodied to the literal bone, they are most likely faking that concussion and you should wake them up and put them back to work.

Kristen

...

Dear Kristen:

I think sacred music gets a bad rap. I'm working on getting it more accepted in the mainstream. Can I send you some of my organ and choral recordings?

Christian Clough
Hamilton, NY

Dear Christian:

You can certainly send it to me, but I will refuse to listen to it. You know why? Because I'm not dead yet! Everyone knows that when you die and go to heaven it's organ and choral music nonstop. You can't get away from it. Even when you go to your heaven hut and slam the cloud door, it's still stuck in your head (which is no longer a human head but a beam of light). I think I'll enjoy this nice variety of music on earth before my sacred playlist kicks off for eternity, thank you.

Kristen

...

Dear Kristen:

I enjoy hamsters but guinea pigs really freak me out. My daughter, however, has her heart set on getting a guinea pig for a pet. Since they are both essentially rodents that live tragically short, wheel-spinning lives, how can I convince her to settle for a hamster instead?

> *Madi Schaefer*
> *Phoenix, AZ*

Dear Madi:

Just put a kitten in a hamster cage and call it a day. She won't care that it's not a guinea pig because kittens are the most adorable creatures in the world and possess a hypnotic power that humans are weak to. As soon as she sees that kitten mew and roll in the sawdust, she'll say, "I love my guinea pig, I'll call him Cider!" Important note: When the kitten inevitably becomes a cat, dispose of him. It's uncomfortable seeing a cat in an aquarium. I guess you are doomed to have the dead pets talk no matter what.

> Kristen

...

Dear Kristen:

Why isn't Pigeon Forge on the national monument registry?

> *Sean Stomsky*
> *Santa Barbara, CA*

Dear Sean:

To protect it from the terrorists. If you don't think that registry is a sweet terrorist checklist, you are living in the summer of 2001, my friend. And I don't want to live in a world where Dollywood is threatened. Worse yet, I might hate it more if the terrorists checked out Dollywood and started going there on a regular vacation basis. I don't want to be standing in line for the Dollyland Grits, Tits, and Adventure ride and have a bunch of eager terrorists cut in front of me. Then I'd have to tell them they were cutting, they'd apologize and explain how excited they were. Then I'd tell them the Baby Jesus Sea Dragon ride is even better, and the next thing you know we're all making babies.

Also, Reba McEntire is in charge of making the registry and everyone knows she's jealous of Dolly.

Kristen

...

Dear Kristen:

I actually do believe that the children are our future. I mean, duh. But here's the thing. The other day I was at the park and I met this baby who I thought was kind of an asshole. I don't want him to be part of my future. I don't want him to be a part of the decision-making process for the United States, or a major corporation or an arts organization. I don't trust this baby. Is there an effective way to encourage this child to go into selling cars or perhaps mattresses?

Shea St. Ives
Cleveland, OH

Dear Shea:

You're making the mistake of thinking that the world is going to be like it is now in the future. Wake up! We are not going to have decisions or arts or the United States. That will be a sweet memory for the olds. Mattresses will be cut up and the springs will be used for scraping tools and we will eat the stuffing to live another day. We are talking three levels below *Mad Max* territory, because we won't be dressed in cool leather outfits straddling mopeds. We will be wearing the only abundant resource available to us: plastic bags. What you see in that asshole baby is the apocalypse. He knows it. That's why he's being such a dick. You'd be a dick too.

Kristen

Louis C.K.

(The editors and Mr. C.K. would like to apologize in advance for his overt and unnecessary hostility. Mr. C.K. was, by his own admission, "having a bad day.")

Dear Louis:
How come Arnold Palmer gets a drink named after him and I don't? Could you recommend steps toward "I have a drink named after me" greatness?

> *Envious Imbiber*
> *Ann Arbor, MI*

Dear Envious:
First of all, the Arnold Palmer, as it is known (half lemonade, half iced tea), was not named after the golfer Arnold

Palmer. It was named after your mother's dried-up old snatchola. Yeah. You heard me right.

Louis

. . .

Dear Louis:
I'm ready to grow a mustache, but I don't want to send the wrong message. What does each style of mustache say about its owner?

Norm
Jacksonville, FL

Dear Norm:
I don't know what any mustache says about its owner, but I know what yours will say. It will say, "Please get me off the face of this stupid, ugly cunt." Nobody likes you. Even the *a* and the *n* at the end of your name ran off because you're such a fucking stupid twat.

Thanks for your letter.
Louis

. . .

Dear Louis:
Is secondhand smoke really as bad as everyone says it is?

Rebekkeh T.
San Francisco, CA

Dear Rebekkeh:

Very good question. Let me give you some statistics.

1. Your name is stupid.
2. Nobody cares what you think.
3. I hate you.
4. I have a pretty nice penis. It's not huge, but it's well sized and it's nice. This isn't directed at you. It's directed at any attractive woman reading this book who might run into me later in her life. I'd rather advertise my penis than answer your stupid question. Idiot.

Louis

. . .

Dear Louis:

For a long time the main thing that's bothered me is procrastination. Like right now. I'm procrastinating instead of doing my job. In the old days humans hunted and were hunted—by mastodons and wolverines and such—but now we sit in front of computers. We got no excitement. So I procrastinate. Piss people off. Barrel through deadlines. Living la vida loca. Am I wrongheaded about all this?

Bret Thurber
Las Vegas, NV

Dear Bret:

You sound like a real card. You sound like you really got a clever mind and you're always spinning your wheels about some-whatsit crazy business. Mastodons??? What a nut. "That Bret," your friends must say, "he is quite a kook. I hope his wife has a baby into his mouth and it gets lodged in his throat and he chokes on his own stupid baby."

Louis

. . .

Dear Louis:
I cut up an old backpack to make my own Baby Björn. He doesn't seem to like it much. Any advice on how to make it more comfortable or entertaining for the kid?

Paula Winchell
Winnipeg, Canada

Dear Paula:
First of all, I don't believe you. I have owned three Baby Björns and I can assure you that you couldn't make one out of a "cut up" old backpack.

Second of all, Baby Björns are stupid. Just carry your ugly, ugly kid or let him walk next to you as you live your shit life. Don't make him hang on your sad, flat, old, pimply, sweater-wearing chest.

Third of all, I hate you because you leave things out of every sentence. "He doesn't seem to like it much." Who?! Who the fuck are you talking about, you lazy cunt?!

"Any advice?" Do you mean, "Do you have any advice?" You left out the "Do you have" part. I hate people who talk like that. They also say things like "Fact is..." Get your goddamn hands out of your pockets and say an entire sentence! And please take the entire town of Winnipeg and shove it up your mom's asshole.

Louis

...

Dear Louis:
I took my baby girl out for a walk last week and a teenage boy passed me in the street and told me I was "a total MILF." What does this mean? Should I be insulted?

Cindy Valdes
Buckhorn, CO

Dear Cindy:
MILF is a common acronym used by teenagers these days. It stands for "Ugly Bitch Who Lies about Some Kid Calling Her a MILF." He didn't say it and you know it. Why don't you tell me the real story? You were taking your baby girl for a walk when nobody walked by and nobody said anything. Because you are invisible to the caring world.

Oh my god. What is wrong with me?

Louis

George Saunders

Dear George:
I've been reading the bible recently and I've found that the more important a character, the greater their capacity for ferocious outbursts of violence against underlings. What gives?

Lorna

Dear Lorna:
How dare you! You dare to question the Lord your God? Ye, Lorna, shall, verily, be smited for your insolence, for your question hath engaged my full wrath! And, as you can see from my incredible fury, I am incredibly important!

Ha, ha, no, seriously: interesting question, Lorna. I think this is because the Bible is an ancient text, i.e., it is not really all that "modern." In our modern times, we know that underlings are best managed with a gentle, loving hand. Like, for example, we don't call them "underlings." We might call them, you know, "Guest Facilitation Associate #43" or "Hey, you there!" or "vassals" or, if we are a little drunk, and they are just out of hearing range, "assholes," pronounced in such a way that it rhymes with "vassals," which, because we are a little drunk and are into Renaissance role play–type games, we find "fair amusing." In those ancient times, when everything was made of either stone or rope, people were generally smaller. Hence it was sometimes necessary to really yell in order to be heard through the tiny, filthy ears then so prevalent. Also, there were no "water filters" or "breast pumps," and dinosaurs roamed the land, freely eating the various Union soldiers and whatnot that were always foraging around. Everything was so different then! I guess what I'm saying is, who are we to judge? The God who reigns eternal now is not necessarily the same God who reigned eternal then. Think of "Adam." Think of "Eve." Do we still believe in them? Or do we mostly just use them in comical television commercials, where Eve wants to buy something extravagant and Adam rolls his eyes and the snake (i.e., "Satan") suddenly sprouts an arm and gives Eve a "thumbs-up"? In any event, who are we to question His approach? Or, as we might say it now, "his approach." My advice is, stop reading the Bible, Lorna. Or maybe stop reading it so closely? Try reading the Bible while checking your e-mail while loading apps on your iPad while breaking up with someone via text while performing microsurgery on a microbot. That will have the effect of making you read less closely, and hence you will find yourself obsessing less about small, unimportant things—such as words, meanings, and inferences that might have repercussions for your immortal soul. Of course, I am just one man, hardly a God at all.

> Hope you found this
> helpful, and bless thee,
> George Saunders

P.S. Actually, I just heard from God Himself, the actual God, via this thing that sometimes happens in my brain, and, turns out, Lorna, your question really "raised His ire." You are indeed going to be smoted, as I threatened above, although just a little bit (and not by me, but by the actual God), and guess what for? For not capitalizing "Bible!" Isn't that something? Who knew? But don't worry: it's going to be like a mini-smiting. (This is not me, this is Him.) He said you might find that the organic spring mix you just bought has gone slightly off? Also, for the next forty-eight hours, your wireless connection is going to be completely unbearable. And He said—I'm quoting directly here— "Tell her to go look for a hidden symbol contained in the fur on the left eyelid of her ferret, Gibran." Does that mean anything to you, Lorna?

P.S.S. Apparently, I am also due a mini-smiting, for making so bold as to comically "imitate" God (see paragraph 1, above). Even though I was just kidding. Turns out, God is pretty literal. See, now I—ouch!—I just now got this terrible rash on my Huh. Interesting. It appears that, as an additional aspect of my mini-smiting, I am now unable to remember the words for various parts of the body. Seems like I am getting a more severe smitage than even you, Lorna. That's what I get, I guess, for offering "advice." Ouch, wow. This really stings. I just leapt to my...what do you call those things at the ends of one's...? Darn it. Anyway, I just leapt to those two things that occur at the end of those two other, longish, pants-clad things, then took my pants off and ran an icy cold bath and submerged myself in it—but to no avail! This rash is still wildly burning my...my...Wow! Ouch! Lorna, honestly, at this point I am so desperate for relief from this pain, and have been racking my...my... that...thinking thing...damn. Damn it. Count yourself lucky, Lorna, that all you have is some wilted spring mix. I envy you with all of my...uh ...

...

Dear George:
I'm looking for a book that I can read on the subway and it'll make all the other commuters look at me with envy, and possibly even think, "Good god, he must be so much smarter than the rest of us. I bet he's got his life together. I want to be his friend." Any recommendations?

F.H.
New York, NY

Dear F.H.:

You know, sometimes these "To the Believer" questions seem like—I don't know—setups or something. That is, they seem to be "ironic" questions designed to prompt "ironic" answers. The questioner asks something facetious, and the responder gives a sort of over-the-top, equally facetious answer. It makes for a sort of tonal monotony, don't you think? That's why I so much appreciate your question, F.H.: I can feel the very real sincerity and good sense behind it—as well as the real need. Haven't we all felt, at some time or another: *Oh, I am so lonely. Life is passing so quickly. If only I knew how to trick someone into loving me?*

Now, the obvious suggestion would be: the Bible. (Or, as Lorna would have it: "the bible.") If you want to really get things cooking, try reading "the bible" on the subway, with red pen in hand. Of course, some people might find this offensive. God, for that matter, might find it offensive. And based on a recent experience I've had with offending God, I'd advise against this, unless you are a big fan of genital rashes. So: ixnay on the Ible-bay. (Clarification: not on the ook-bay itself, but, rather, on the idea of arking-may up the Ible-bay with a ed-ray en-pay. Enough aid-say?)

Speaking of which, as a courtesy, may I point out that, in your question, you failed to capitalize the "g" in "God," F.H.? (Or as God might now refer to you, just before He sends down your genital rash: "f.h.")

Anyway, F.H., if you're really intent on meeting the sort of people who decide they'd like to meet you via assessing the type of book you're reading on the subway (!), try one of the following recent publications:

Common Problems of the Very Wealthy,
Well-Endowed, and Omniscient

Why Can't I Stop Loving So Selflessly, and
Being Such an Incredible Cook?

Or, if you want, try a more "ornery, contrarian" approach:

Eyes Up, Moronic Commuter! There's a
Whole Beautiful World Out There!

What Are You Looking at My Book for, When a Guy
with Advanced-Stage TB Is About to Cough
Down Your Neck?

Stop Scanning My Book Cover, Asshole,
or I Swear to God on the Holy Bible...

Or, my personal favorite:

Care to Make Love in That Gross Little Space Between Cars?

Best of luck in your search
for authentic friendship
and love,
George Saunders

...

Dear George:

I am the editor of a small but mighty (watch out, Believer*!) 'zine that publishes independent writers' and artists' great work. As a lot of new writers are still . . . developing . . . their style, we get a lot of crappy writing. Being a volunteer, word-of-mouth, grassroots project, how can we tell people, "Your piece is awful so we won't be printing it," while keeping our reputation as a great bunch of kindly people?*

> *Veronica*
> *Glendale, CA*

Hi Veronica:

One obvious approach is to accept everything you are sent, and only run the pieces you like. When an author inquires, just say, "Yours is our favorite piece of all time. We are running it in the very next issue." Then keep doing that, until too many angry people are dropping by/calling. Then move to a new location. Of course, this takes a lot of work. But nobody ever said great art would be easy. Anyway, I have taken the liberty of drafting up a few form rejection letters you might want to try:

> *Dear NAME,*
>
> *Although we cower collectively at the power of your wanton pro-duction, we fear the lancing blade of your cutting prosody may too effectively skewer the banal sensibilities of the scant, nominal*

*readership (Hi, Mom!) we have heretofore procured, and hence,
we return forthwithal your missal, sans regrets, as well as best
wishes, in terms of your future endeavors d'letter, in all things!*
                    Salud y Bonhomme!
                    Small Glendale 'Zine

Or try this:

Dear NAME,
This is far too "good" for us. Please send it to The Believer.
                    All the best,
                    Small Glendale 'Zine

Or this:

Dear NAME,
*You have recently submitted a short story or poem to the editors of
the Small Glendale 'Zine. Although your work had undeniable
merit, we regret to inform you that these heroic young people are
no more. All eight of them perished while attempting to rescue a
group of beautiful, angelic, utterly innocent orphans drowning in
the notoriously dangerous Glendale Rapids. The editors were on
a sort of outing... yes, an outing raising money for international
AIDS awareness. Also, hepatitis. They were really a super bunch.
Until the drowning. What a loss that whole drowning deal was
for the literary/philanthropic community. What a handsome/
pretty/sexy, and nice—very nice, very considerate—group they
were. Prior to the drowning. Also, come to think of it, even during*

the drowning. From what we've heard. They kept deferring to one another, using lots of ironic indie movie references, until the last editor had expired. They were just, in short, prior to that tragic drowning incident (from which, by the way, all of the orphans emerged alive, and even dry, due to the incredible courage of those editors, especially Veronica), a great bunch of kindly people, who will be sorely missed around Glendale and would have, in all probability, accepted your manuscript, had they not, as described above, drowned, forever and for all time, never to return, or even glance at their slush pile, for all eternity. So if you still have something you want read, we suggest you send it to The Believer.

All the best,

Current (Saddened) Residents of the Very Office That Formerly Housed the Small Glendale 'Zine.

George

Zach Galifianakis

Dear Zach:
I think I understand what dogs are saying. I don't have a dog, but there are a lot in my neighborhood. Is this possible or am I crazy?
Jed Resick
Brooklyn, NY

Dear Jed:
You could really help a lot of people if this is the case. Is it not worth exploring? Meaning, shouldn't you volunteer yourself to a university study on the subject? You must take this seriously. I feel like my family dog, a golden retriever named Zorba, would have loved to have a human translator. Looking back, I imagine it would've gone like this:

ZORBA (*in a translated bark*): I ain't interested in fetching no more tennis balls.

ME: Throw some more and see if he gets it.

ZORBA: I got to figure out how to get into the house. I feel a cold front moving in from the west.

ME: Zorba's coat is so thick, he is fine out in the snow.

ZORBA: Jesus Christ, this family is thick. How long do I have to bark before they let me in the basement that is only two degrees warmer?

ME: I am going to take you to the apple festival, Zorba, so everyone will want to pet you and you can wag your tail to show how happy you are.

ZORBA: That tail wagging is a nervous tic. I got some sort of dog diabetes going on and you mistake it for happiness. Does it not make you wonder why my testicles are the size of bocce balls?

Zach

...

Dear Zach:
I really should see a dermatologist, but I just don't have the time (or health insurance). What's the difference between a good mole and a bad mole?

E. Jackson
Melbourne, FL

Dear E.:

Location, really. It all depends on where it is. One on the eyelid is not good. One in the mouth is not good. The anus is not a bad place to have one but showing it off causes a problem. A good place is on the face. A small one on the cheek is classy and expresses a worldliness that you do not get from a wart. If you do have one on the face, make sure that it is hairless, seeing as haired moles went out of fashion after the Renaissance but are still fashionable at Renaissance festivals. I once had a mole on the right side of my chin as a youth and my mother decided to freeze it off, fearing that it would grow into something that looked like a burnt silver-dollar pancake. I regret that thing is gone. It defined me. I was eight years old but because of that mole I could get away with smoking a pipe and no one would even care. So, location.

Zach

...

Dear Zach:

How did the wishbone become the wishbone? It's kind of gross that it's in the turkey's neck. Maybe you could start a tradition with the wish potato peel. That sounds more humane and animal friendly. People's wishes should not depend on a turkey's mortality. What do you think?

Emily Hache
Dudley, GA

Dear Emily:

I agree that using an animal's body part for your own hopes and dreams is a bit cruel. But the potato idea is one of the worst sentences I have ever read in my adult life. It makes no sense. How are people going to make a tradition out of that? First, a lot of people like eating potato peels. I certainly do. Second, even if people got onboard with it and society agreed to this, you would see revolts in the streets out of frustration over exactly what the physical mechanics are of manipulating a potato peel. Do you rip it? Wave it around? Place it on someone's forehead and say to yourself, "All I wish for is to make all my Camry payments this year"? I need more specifics as to how to pull this off. It is a horrible thing you have come up with and I shall go find and kill a turkey and make a wish on its neckline that you offer a full apology to potatoes and, frankly, turkeys for what a stir you have caused.

Zach

...

Dear Zach:

If push comes to shove I'd choose green, but I really like more of a bluish green. And you?

Olivia Rabe
Charleston, SC

Dear Olivia:
Your name reminds me of the type of green I like: olive. Olive green is the greatest of colors. Blue-green reminds me of an NFL team that nobody likes.

Zach

. . .

Dear Zach:
How on earth does one change one's name without a social security card? I've been getting the runaround from the government and thought I'd try an alternative source for guidance.

Ralph Fines (but not the
Ralph Fiennes)
Beacon Hill, MA

Dear Ralph Fines:
Ralph, you have a good name. *Ralph.* Fines is not bad either. What are your plans? If I were you, I would simply add an "s" and an "e" to your already last name. Ralph Finesse could become a motto for a sports club you decide to open. But let me give it to you this way: Do you think Mr. T, Shelia E, Hulk Hogan, Captain Kangaroo, or Teddy Roosevelt ever needed approval from the American government to change their names? No, they just did it. Start calling yourself something and insist your family, friends, and coworkers start calling you exactly what you want. Trust

me, it will catch on. For a while I was calling myself "Adam Zapple" and people liked it. They respected it. Only later, when I decided to get into show business, did I decide to change it back to Zach Galifianakis.

Zach

Jerry Stahl

Dear Jerry:

My husband has really let himself go. But now our son looks EXACTLY like my husband when we got married. What should I do about all these confusing feelings about my son/husband clone?

Love,
Ophelia

Dear Ophelia:

In the words of your bro Hamlet, "Get thee to a nunnery, why wouldst thou be a breeder of sinners!" I'm not sure how exactly this relates to your question, but I was an English major, and there just aren't a lot of life situations that let me dip into my wide-ranging stock of Shakespeare quotes. As for your son, I'm sure he's a handsome devil, and I would simply advise—be discreet. Otherwise, to quote the bard, "As flies to wanton boys, are we to the gods; they kill us for their sport." Again, not particularly relevant. But—did I mention? I was an English major.

Jerry

. . .

Dear Jerry:
Trivial Pursuit has a "greatest hits" edition? Isn't that just lazy—reusing old trivia?

Sam Billingsworth
Philadelphia, PA

Dear Sam:
Board games? Really, Sam? What happened—burglars break in and steal Parcheesi from the rest home rec room? Sorry, Philly-dog, I'm the wrong man for this question. I associate board games with nights when Grandma baby-sat and I had to breathe in her weird mustard smell, and Christmases when Dad was so broke he got us gifts from the bargain bin at St. Vincent de Paul. (Where every puzzle was missing a piece.) Sorry to let my personal history affect my response, but we can't escape our past, can we, Sam? You don't like it, there's this new thing called a computer. Buy one and Google "Trivial Pursuit greatest hits." I'm sure somebody's blogged about this. There

are a lot of people who never have sex. It's nothing to be ashamed of.

Jerry

. . .

Dear Jerry:
Is the shape of the peanut the most efficient and cushiony shape for shipping packages? Wouldn't spheres or tiny triangles be better?
Ron Sutton
Pinkney, MI

Dear Ron:
The origin of the packing peanut might surprise you. The "peanut" mold was originally developed by Brigham Nance, a cosmetic surgeon from Bountiful, Utah, who lost his testicles in a freak dog bite incident. Dr. Nance believed that Styrofoam peanuts would be a perfect replacement. Sadly, the peanuts—while easy to work with—proved an irritant when placed "*dans le scrotay*," as the French say. Abandoning his dream of "peanuticles," Dr. Nance stashed his molds in his garage. There they remained for decades, until the doctor's grandson, a plucky, overweight ten-year-old with Asperger's syndrome and an unexplained passion for "packing play," found the molds and went to work. Fast-forward and, well, I don't have to tell you, Ron. That hefty, autistic preteen grew up to become the father of modern packing

material. If I send a Ming vase to you in Pinkney (do you get many of those?), chances are you'll pull that priceless little guy out of the box and a whole bunch of styro-nuts will tumble out with him. Anyway, I've kind of rambled here, Ron, so I'm going to skip the sphere and triangle stuff. Let's just say, thanks to a troubled autistic lad, and a rabid beagle in Utah, peanuts got the job.

Jerry

...

Dear Jerry:
I Tweet, I Facebook, I Tumblr, but I have an AOL e-mail. Someone told me I'm out of touch with technology. Is that true? Is AOL passé?

Christian Luciano
Portland, OR

Dear Christian:

Au contraire. You happen to be on the cutting edge of the RSNR (retro social network revolution, for you lames). But don't stop at AOL. Get yourself a taste of a little thing called the U.S. Mail. Sure, Tumblr's configurable post queue can automatically publish your posts on a designated interval. But what about "licking stamps"? You know what I'm saying, Christian. Now back to work—and give my best to your siblings, Li'l Jew and Muslim. I love those guys!

Jerry

...

Dear Jerry:
Have you tried Triscuits and cottage cheese? It's awesome and I
think it should be more popular.

>   *Scott Leggett*
>   *Knoxville, TN*

Dear Scott:

Gee, aren't you the nutritional wild man! But why limit
yourself to cottage cheese? How about graham crackers
and lard? Doritos and borscht? Or—hey, let your hair
down!—Pop-Tarts and guano? Seriously, Scott, I don't
know whether *The Believer*'s reader base lives in a world of
horrific nutritional and recreational deprivation, or I've just
drawn the dregs of the advice bucket. Either way, go 'head,
get your Triscuits on. Be a sport and munch 'em in bed!
The ladies love that. Trust me. Crumb it up, stud puddin'.

>   Jerry

...

Dear Jerry:
I love muffin tops on the ladies, but my girlfriend is stick skinny.
Is there a sexy way I can ask her to grow one?

>   *F. Henderson*
>   *Brooklyn, NY*

Dear F.:

Give it up. You're in Brooklyn, not Milwaukee. If your special someone doesn't want to pack on the lard ledges, you can't make her grow any. No, my friend, your best bet is to go the prosthetic route and buy some stick-ons. They're doing wonderful things with nonchafe adhesive faux fat rings. (Kind of looks like a big flesh-tone Life Saver.) Just wait till your little Olive Oyl turns in for the night, then clamp on those port-o-muffins and—*voilà!*—you've just given your anorexic honey the body of a beer-drunk biker with a spare tire. That's livin', F. Even in Brooklyn.

Jerry

Bob Powers

Dear Bob:
What should I know before I ever step foot in a Pinkberry?
                              Sara
                              Bethesda, MD

Dear Sara:
I'm glad you asked, Sara, because if you tried to pull this off without first checking out the details, you could have very well ended up dead. The first rule of going to Pinkberry: Don't get dead.

The problem with your question is that it's the wrong one. When it comes to Pinkberry, it's not what you know, it's who. And the who you need to know is a motherfucker named Stacey Langan-Hobbs, wife of Dr. Laurence Hobbs, DDS. If you're thinking about hitting up a Pinkberry for the first time, you don't go looking for Stacey Langan-Hobbs. Stacey Langan-Hobbs comes looking for *you*.

She might've already found you. She might be watching you right now, while you read this, watching the curl of your pretty pink lips through her gunsight, wishing she could touch a fingertip to those lips and then carry your kiss in her palm for as long as she can go without washing her hands. She might be observing you day in and day out, wishing she could write you a letter just to tell you she likes the way you smile at people when they get on the same elevator as you. Stacey Langan-Hobbs is probably staying up late at night, pictures of you scattered all over her kitchen table, wondering how she ended up married to the good Dr. Laurence Hobbs when she could have been spending all these years with someone like Sara of Bethesda.

"God dammit, why do I always get my heart wrapped up in this business," Stacey Langan-Hobbs will chastise herself, just before wiping all those pictures of you into the trash. Then she'll pull the ski mask over her head and go out to her car to kill every last son of a bitch who needs killing in order to pave the road between you and your nearest Pinkberry with enough blood to guarantee a smooth drive. In the morning you'll wake up with a handwritten note in your hand that reads, "You're ready, Sara."

> Also, Pinkberry sells
> frozen yogurt.
> Regrets,
> Bob

. . .

Dear Bob:
What is it already?! Who? Or whom? I can't take it anymore!!!
Erica Milner
University of Iowa

Dear Erica:

You use "who" when you're talking about people (human or animated). You use "whom" when you're talking about androids or celebrities. You use "wholmem" when you're referring to the woman your father left you and your mom for when you were six; also, delivery people. Use "whelghm" for when you are telling a story about a childhood friend who changed the way you see things, but whelghm you eventually outgrew and stopped hanging out with, something you still feel kind of guilty about because you're this big, fancy, academic living on her pretty Iowa campus while your childhood bestie is still stuck in the sticks, probably married to god knows whuphlm, doing god knows what just to get her head to her pillow every single night. Use "whuphlm" for the kind of no-good townie your childhood friend probably settled for when she didn't see any other bright lights on the horizon. And use "whieux" when referring to legendary ice hockey forward Mario Lemieux.

Love,

Bob

· · ·

Dear Bob:
What's the perfect formula for deskunking a cat who escaped a few
days ago and got into a spot of trouble?
                                    Rob H.
                                    Geneva, WI

Dear Rob:

I used to chase perfection. I wanted the perfect house. The perfect job. The perfect family. The perfect collection of commemorative shot glasses from all the Big 10 schools, and, yes, even the perfect cat deskunking formula. Then one day I was visited by a ghost who told me, "Take it from me, the only thing perfect in life is death. There are no 'almosts' about death. No way to be kind of dead or a runner-up to someone who's deader than you. Death is blanket, unending, unblinking perfection. Life is about flailing wildly amidst the imperfections hitting you from every which way. You want perfect, you might as well die. You wanna live, you need to loosen up. Take it from me— I'm a ghost."

So loosen up, Rob. Take it from me, I'm a guy ghosts like to talk to sometimes.

                                    With a heavy heart,
                                    Bob

· · ·

Dear Bob:

VNTY PL8S R 4 DCKHDS. AM I WRNG?

Anonymous

Dear Anonymous:

Yesterday my wife and I were driving behind a car that bore the vanity plate "SKN DOC." I had recently discovered a strange growth on my lower back and I was very worried, so I had my wife speed up to "SKN DOC," certain that he must be a dermatologist. While she was honking her horn, I removed my shirt and hung my bare torso out the window while pointing to the growth. Rather than offer me some help, SKN DOC merely sped up his car. I'd like to think he was on his way to an emergency dermatology appointment of some kind, but I'm afraid the more likely assumption is the one you make, Anonymous. Namely that VNTY PL8S R, quite simply, 4 DCKHDS.

Yours in Christ,

Bob

. . .

Dear Bob:

For the last two days I've been applying a poultice of bleach and flour to a wine-stained granite countertop. I feel like an idiot. It's so not working. Do you have a better solution?

Tanya Cogdon

Orlando, FL

Dear Tanya:

I once had a party that got a little out of hand. There were a lot of people there, including one celebrity athlete whieux shall remain nameless. Long story short, the next morning I woke up with my kitchen covered in broken glass and my elephant tusk countertops stained to the marrow with Côtes du Rhône. I was about to resort to some tough-on-the-environment cleansers when my celebrity athlete friend calmed me down and told me that there's another way.

"Witchcraft," he said.

Having been a practitioner of the dark arts since before his first Stanley Cup win, he proceeded to cast a spell on my countertops that made that stain lift from my countertop and turn to a dark, shrieking cloud that seemed to bear the face of my grandfather. I opened the window to shoo the cloud away and—*poof*—that stain was gone for good. So throw away that poultice and hit the bars until you bag yourself a professional athlete who is well versed in the ways of witchcraft.

> Doing it to them before
> they do it to us,
> Bob

...

Dear Bob:

I bought a level as I was told it's good for a variety of things. So far the pictures are all straight in my house. But now what? I'm not a builder of anything. Are there any other practical purposes to this tool?

> *Smith Jones*
> *Little Rock, AR*

Dear Smith:

I'm gonna level with ya. BANG! Was that awesome or what? Throw me a softball, why don'tcha?

But seriously, I want to give you a straight answer. I'm just not sure if your letter is on the level. KAZOW! Like a machine over here!

Sorry, I'm sure you don't have all day to wait for me to give you an answer. I mean, some of us have to work. We can't all sit around all day listening to our favorite '80s UK pop band Level 42. HOLY SHIT, HE DID IT AGAIN!

Okay, okay, Smith. I'm sorry about all the joking. Thing is, I'm not sure what a level is and I was just stalling, hoping there'd be some kind of terrible apocalyptic event that would make this question, and my answer, meaningless. That didn't happen and I've let you down. I feel terrible and it's your fault. Sleep well with that.

> Go to hell,
> Bob

The Pleasure Syndicate

Dear Pleasure Syndicate:
Is there anywhere God can't see you?

Sandra
Rochester, NY

Dear Sandra:
Short answer: no. There is no place in the universe, no location in time, no conceivable space to occupy where the Almighty cannot see you. He can see you in your home, He can see you before protons existed, He can see you on a bike. However, you might take some small consolation in the fact that God is deaf in one ear and might miss something you say depending on which side of His head you're standing.

Yours,
Pleasure Syndicate

...

Dear Pleasure Syndicate:
Can you explain to me the "brilliance" of Joni Mitchell? I want to like her—I really do—but I just don't get it.

> *Janet*
> *Pittsburgh, PA*

Dear Janet:
Don't get it? What is wrong with you? Are your ears filled with cement? I don't know what sort of brute you are, but I do know that in just a couple of short sentences, you've somehow managed to display the kind of ignorance usually reserved for people who think dice are edible. It's a good thing you're wearing three Slipknot masks at once, because I don't know how you could stand the sight of your face in the mirror.

 Joni Mitchell's the one that sings "Big Yellow Taxi," right?

> Pleasure Syndicate

...

Dear Pleasure Syndicate:
What is the difference between sexual and sensual? Is there even one?

> *Bradley*
> *Tulane University*
> *New Orleans, LA*

Dear Bradley:

You can think of "sexual" as a way to describe actual carnal behavior—intercourse, oral sex, paying someone to put on clogs and kick you in the testicles. "Sensual" has overtones of sexuality but is broader in application, e.g., a sensual massage, a tango class taught by a real-life Spanish person, a long winter evening with *The Best of Lenny Kravitz* on the turntable. And, by the way, the two terms are not mutually exclusive: a cucumber used for vaginal penetration is being used sexually, while a cucumber onstage performing a striptease is engaging in a sensual performance.

Pleasure Syndicate

...

Dear Pleasure Syndicate:

Here's a problem that I have, and I hope you can help: my mother-in-law lives with my husband and me. Okay, not a problem, per se. But I found her going through my clothes drawers the other night when I walked upstairs and she wasn't aware of my presence. What in the hell?! Should I say something to my husband? At the time, I just walked out, pretending not to see, and I don't even think my mother-in-law knows that I know!

Elaine

Jackson, MS

Dear Elaine:

Have you ever attended a production of the musical *Pippin*? In this delightful fable, a young lad comes down from the mountains, where he lives with the cloud people, to a small village called Brigadoon. He steals a crust of bread and is persecuted by an angry police ogre named Shrek, all the while falling in love with a beautiful young mermaid named Chastity. There are some lively and heartfelt musical numbers throughout (one is sung by a giant candelabra named Studs), and everyone leaves with huge grins on their faces. My guess is that your mother-in-law was probably looking in your drawer for tickets to this show. Why don't you throw down a few dollars and take her to see a production of it at your neighborhood performing arts center? I think it would be a terrific bonding experience for the two of you!

Sincerely,

Pleasure Syndicate

...

Dear Pleasure Syndicate:

There never seem to be enough hours in the day. I can never get caught up. Any suggestions on time management?

Not Enough Time on My

Hands

Dear Not Enough Time on Your Hands:

Time is a slippery, slippery beast. Did you know that the ancient Egyptians used to count the days by the rising and setting of the sun? Wild stuff. My suggestion to you would be to buy a simple, inexpensive spiral notebook (most likely your local drugstore will have a small selection of them located near the peanut brittle and shoe polish), and on each page write a name of the day of the week. This way you'll always know the names of the days of the week without having to commit them to memory, and you can use the time you would have spent trying to remember them on some other task, such as organizing your pornographic Hummel collection.

Best of luck!

Pleasure Syndicate

. . .

Dear Pleasure Syndicate:

What sort of superheroes do you think get laid the most? The flying or swimming kind?

Sasha

Pittsburgh, PA

Dear Sasha:

The flying kind. Perhaps you can tell me this: What sort of Sasha gets laid the most? The male or female kind?

Best Regards,

Pleasure Syndicate

...

Dear Pleasure Syndicate:
I cut my own hair, but my boyfriend thinks I should have it done
by a professional. Should I spend the money? What does a salon
know about haircutting that I don't?

Thanks for your time.
Sally B.
Chicago, IL

Dear Sally B.:
The word "salon" dates back to the seventeenth century, but it wasn't actually used to describe a beauty parlor until around 1913. That's not even that long ago! People have been cutting their own hair for much longer than that. It's called instinct, Sally. Wild animals use it to hunt and trap fish. It's the reason babies can stand up straight and then touch their toes without any prompting from Mom or Dad. We humans instinctually know how to cut our own hair. Trust that. Any so-called "professional" in the field of hair-cutting is just a modern-day snake oil salesman as far as I'm concerned.

You're beautiful, Sally. Don't let your boyfriend tell you differently.

Keep cutting!
Pleasure Syndicate

P.S. Next time, please include a photo of yourself.

...

Dear Pleasure Syndicate:
Bloodstains out of pajamas? Any advice?
                              Keenan

Dear Keenan:

The simple answer would be to use a specialty product, like Procter & Gamble's JammySplotch brand De-Blooding Powder (the authors recommend "Original Scent"). But why seek an elegant solution? After all, there was nothing elegant about how you got blood on your pajamas in the first place! Instead, try something complicated and a bit disturbing. Perhaps you could bring your blood-stained pajamas to a car wash run by youth soccer players trying to raise money for a new set of mesh scrimmage jerseys. Ask whichever child is operating the hose if you can "snag that for a sec, chief," then, blocking the hose nozzle with your thumb, spray an explosive blast directly onto the stain from a distance of one or two inches. Next, yell for the child with the scrubbing brush to come over and "do what he's paid to do." When the stain has been lightened to your satisfaction, thank the children for the use of their resources, inform them that it "must be their lucky day," and toss a fistful of sweaty singles into their donation box. *Voilà!*

                              Pleasure Syndicate

. . .

Dear Pleasure Syndicate:
I've heard that the word "can't" should be a part of one's vocabu-
lary. Any other words?

Ben

Dear Ben:

Most magazines and newspapers in America are written
at a sixth-grade reading level. (Excluding *The New Yorker,*
whose staff is so dumb they think "focused" is spelled with
two *s*'s and they have to ask their readers to write their car-
toon captions for them! Sixth grade? They wish!) In other
words, to qualify as reasonably literate, one's vocabulary
should include every single word in common usage among
sixth graders, with special attention paid to the parts of
speech called "8's" (h8r, l8r, Ruth B8r, etc.). Best to memo-
rize some teenage sex slang, too, for conversational flavor,
or to banter with in the bleachers at midnight basketball
games. Of course, if keeping up with the ever evolving
argot of the tween set seems too daunting a task, you may
simply want to pepper your speech with occasional youth-
ful declarations like "Sk8r boiz rule" or "My obsession with
collecting anatomically correct dolls has jeopardized my
marriage, my health, and my job as a counselor for troubled
teens."

Pleasure Syndicate

...

Dear Pleasure Syndicate:
The time has come to put my folks in a nursing home. They're both
forgetful and they're both at risk for injury. This makes me sad,
but I don't think it can wait much longer. What's the best way to
"sell" them on this idea?

Lucy Overgaard
Stockholm, Sweden

Dear Lucy:
This is a heartbreaking situation, and one that's become
common in our age of improved medical care, rising life
expectancies, and ungrateful brat children who care more
for their Nook reading pads than for the people who beat
Hitler. There are no easy ways to convince elderly parents to give up their independence for assisted living, only
hard ways and harder ways, plus a way known as "The
Boggs-Hurley Geriatric Extraction Technique," which, trust
us, you don't have the stomach for. But it goes without
saying that whatever your chosen method, it should be
based on persuasion, not coercion. If your own powers of
persuasion are lacking, you might want to hire a celebrity
spokesperson to speak in your stead, preferably someone
who is trusted by senior citizens, such as Wilford Brimley,
Tommy Lasorda, or one of the lesser-known Baldwin brothers. Imagine the twinkle of joy in your mother or father's
eye when, for instance, Brucie Baldwin comes dancing up

their front steps, his long, lanky hoofer's frame as spry as ever, to doff his top hat and suggest that they "read those brochures for Quail Haven Village your daughter keeps slipping into your large-print word-finder books—whatya say, old-timer?"!

Pleasure Syndicate

Dave Eggers

Dear Dave:

*When did it become so uncool to call yourself a singer-songwriter?
Is there another way to describe what I do that won't have people
rolling their eyes quite so much?*

T.Y.

Charleston, SC

Dear T.Y.:

How about yodeler? You could call what you do yodeling,
and people would be impressed. Yodeling has always been a
serious and honored line of work. Did you know Presidents
McKinley and Truman were both yodelers? They were so
respected by everyone, too! So that's one option: call yourself a yodeler, then be president. Or you could just change

it up a bit. Instead of singer-songwriter, you could say you're a screamer-scribbler. That's accurate enough—I trust you can't actually sing—and gives it an edge, doesn't it? Or you could say that you're curing lupus. Then you'd really have people's respect. You can tell your friends, "Hey, everyone! Come down to the Thirsty Cactus, where, after paying a three-dollar cover, you can watch me and my acoustic guitar cure lupus." People will think you're some kind of god. Until you start singing. But by then you'd already have a sweet eighteen bucks in your pocket. That's called f-you money.

Happy to help,
Dave

. . .

Dear Dave:

I've got a lot of rage issues, and now that I'm fifty, I don't have the same outlets I did when I was younger. Contact sports and mosh pits in clubs just lead to broken bones and even more rage. What's an old dude to do?

Old Fogey
Austin, TX

Dear Old Fogey:
You should take it easy. You're not the man you once were, and no one—including you—should expect you to be the

same person. How about having a seat on the couch? How about watching a movie? Have you seen *Logan's Run*?

Dave

. . .

Dear Dave:

I'm pregnant and I can't stop drinking Fanta orange soda. I wouldn't call it a craving as much as a calling. It's fantastic. Will I lose my taste for it after the kid is born? And if so, does that mean it's really my unborn son who has the insatiable craving for orange soda?

Kristi Worthington
Roy, PA

Dear Kristi:

I, too, love orange soda. I don't buy much of it here, but everywhere else in the world you go, you see Fanta, and it's invariably the best option. But what's in Fanta? No one knows. I called them one time and asked them, and they chewed me out pretty bad. Thank you for asking about Fanta. You made my day. Have you seen *Logan's Run*?

Dave

. . .

Dear Dave:

I think my boyfriend has more than just a literary crush on Sheila Heti, which is troublesome since her latest book is all about blow jobs AND because my boyfriend and I are attending a workshop that she's teaching this weekend. How should I act at the workshop?

> *Sindee M.*
> *Chicago, IL*

Dear Sindee:

Well, I got your letter a few months after you attended that workshop with Sheila. And Sheila says the whole thing was a disaster. Your boyfriend was ogling her the whole time, and then he said that creepy thing about how he likes to wash himself in the backyard, with the watering can and the trowel. A lot of people asked for their money back, and I guess you guys are banned from attending any more workshops, huh? Sindee, why do you keep ruining things in these cities you move to? You did the same thing in Milwaukee. And Columbus before that. Why do you want to ruin workshops? Why not be people who don't ruin workshops?

> Yrs,
> Dave

. . .

Dear Dave:

If granola is supposed to be so good for you, then why is it just as fattening as a cupcake? I'd rather eat the cupcake and call it a day. I'm willing to compromise with a "healthy" cupcake like carrot or something if that will even things out. What do you think?

P. Lydon

Delray Beach, FL

Dear P. Lydon:

Is Office Depot still headquartered in Delray Beach? Are office supplies cheaper down there? You'd think you'd get some kind of discount. But don't buy furniture there; the furniture is terrible—all made of particle board with cheap veneers. And yet I like shopping at Office Depot. The aisles are so wide, the ceilings so high. I always buy something I don't need. And sometimes, while wandering too long in those wide aisles, unsure what I want and what I need, I wonder what I'm doing there at all, when I could be in Delray Beach, with you.

Yrs,

Dave

...

Dear Dave:

I live alone and would really like a pet for companionship. But I'm also completely irresponsible and likely to forget to feed it for days

if not weeks. (Isn't my honesty and self-awareness refreshing?)
What's the best pet for me?

Eric Anderson
Winston-Salem, NC

Dear Eric:

A pet will bring you great joy and companionship, but sometimes pets will eat the toes and fingers of small children. Do you have children? Seems like every few months there's a story about a couple waking up to the screaming of their baby, only to find that their pet ferret has eaten the baby's toes and fingers. Which is a terrible thing all around, because surely the couple had no idea that the ferret would do such a thing. They wanted a pet, and probably felt that the baby would enjoy the company of such a pet. Indeed, in the same spirit of generosity, they allowed the ferret to roam the house uncaged—all decisions born of love, not negligence. And yet then the ferret does a terrible thing. This says something about the law of unintended consequences. And it says to me that you should not get a pet. You should be alone. Don't talk to people, because they might upset you, and you them. Don't buy plastics. Best not to move too much, lest you do irreparable harm to those you love and the world at large.

Dave

. . .

Dear Dave:

Can a broken heart literally kill you? I'm telling you, man, it seriously feels like it. Should I get one of those stress tests at the hospital just to be on the safe side?

> *Phil*
> *Glendale, CA*

Dear Phil:

Have you considered getting a pet?

> Yrs,
> Dave

Amy Sedaris

Dear Amy:

Last summer, my wife and I inherited three hermit crabs from her eight-year-old nephew when he went to camp. It's been six months and we're still stuck crabsitting. I'm worried that if I flush them down the toilet, they'll morph into supersized megacrabs, crawl back through the pipes, and seek revenge. What's the best way to "take care" of a hermit crab?

Eric J. Fetterman
New York, NY

P.S. Do you have any interest in three hermit crabs? They don't take up much space.

Dear Eric:

"Taking care" of a hermit crab is a delicate operation. Hermit crabs are an unruly sort, possessing a large pincer and—believe you me—they're just waiting for a chance to clamp that claw into a major artery in your neck. Never turn your back on a hermit crab. Now, the first thing you have to do is coax the crab out of its shell. I suggest either using a piece of meat or appealing to the crab's ceaseless and fanatical lust for the opposite sex. This second option would require you to either provide a decoy or act as a decoy. Once the crab is out of its shell, pounce. Bring the wrath of God down upon the crab's tiny and spongy exoskeleton in the form of a large brick. Make sure you are accurate with your first blow, because the last thing you want on your hands is an agitated hermit crab.

Amy

P.S. Thank you for your generous offer, but after spending last July at a three-day jazz festival, where I shacked up in a makeshift lean-to with a percussionist I just met named Zobo, I already have more crabs than I could possibly care for.

. . .

Dear Amy:
Why isn't anyone worried about me?

An Inquiring Mom
Readfield, Maine

P.S. I asked this question of my daughter just minutes ago, and she suggested your column as a place to air my concerns about myself.

Dear Mom:

This is a tough one. I wish I could say that nobody is worried about you because you are so well grounded and capable, but we both know deep in our hearts that that is a lie. It's pretty clear that you are a train on the verge of derailment. You are a speeding vehicle and the wheels have come off. So, why doesn't anybody care? Could it be that your existence barely registers as a blip on the human-awareness scale? As Occam's razor states, the simplest explanation is the best. I suppose a better question to consider than "Why isn't anyone worried about me?" might be "How can I exact a horrible revenge on my thoughtless offspring?" There's a question I can sink my fangs into.

Amy

...

Dear Amy:

I want to make a bong. I have some old flower vases and some duct tape, but I want it to look cute. What can you suggest to help me?

Maggie Smith
St. Paul, MN

Dear Maggie Smith from St. Paul:

So you want to make a bong, do you? For those of you who either don't know what a bong is or are employed by the DEA, I'll explain what Maggie Smith from St. Paul is asking about. This "bong" that Maggie Smith from St. Paul speaks of is a water pipe that one might use to smoke an illegal substance such as marijuana or hashish. As I'm sure Maggie Smith from St. Paul already knows, by using a bong one is able to slam a bigger hit, or suck a major toke, and you know it's smooth, baby, cooled by the water, you've got your finger on the carburetor hole and you're suckin' on that pipe until the sweet bowl is cashed... or something like that. Anyway, I'm not sure why Maggie Smith from St. Paul would be asking me about a bong, and I'm pretty sure it's equally confusing to my parole officer, but I'll give it a shot.

Try painting a skull on it. Whatever.

Amy

. . .

Dear Amy:

Recently, my partner and I decided to become vegetarians. As a general rule we have decided not to eat anything that once had eyes, including fish, animals, and birds. My question is with scallops. Since they seem to have no eyes or central nervous systems, I am wondering if they feel pain when caught and prepared for human consumption. Is it ethical to consume mollusks on a vegetarian diet?

> *Gary Brewer*
> *Mesa, AZ*

Dear Gary:

No eyes, Gary? No nervous system? Well, I bet that's news to this sturdy little bivalve shellfish. I don't know what type of sick fantasy world you and your partner are attempting to construct, but I'm guessing it's a calculated effort to purposely remain naive in order that you two can continue to indulge in the demented barbarism you so casually refer to as "consume." I think you're the one who lives in a shell, Gary.

> Amy

...

Dear Amy:

I've worked at a nursing home and have encountered a stinky nuisance. Is there a name for the certain substance that accumulates between folds of skin, like you might find on a morbidly obese person? Is it simply called "fold cheese"?

> *Rebeka Miller*
> *Flushing, MI*

Dear Rebeka:

Absolutely it's called "fold cheese" and thanks for asking. The interesting thing about fold cheese is how conservative people get when serving it. Don't be content plopping it on a cracker or layering it on top of a burger. That barely scratches the surface. What about fondue? Remember, when harvesting fold cheese, the deeper you get, the more robust! So don't be afraid to really get in there.

Amy

. . .

Dear Amy:

I recently purchased a collection of sea monkeys. They are supposed to be "the world's greatest pets." On the booklet that accompanied the aquarium, it illustrates sea monkeys with the ability to dance, create government, and a plethora of other tasks. Unfortunately, my sea monkeys don't do anything but float in the aquarium. Is it outrageous to want my pets to do things that other pets do with their owners?

Christopher M. Lippa
Brighton, Massachusetts

Dear Christopher:

No, I don't think it's outrageous to expect your pets (or your children, for that matter) to excel. Often the key is discipline. Sure, your brine shrimp spend the day floating in the bowl, but that's only because you're reinforcing this behavior. It's time for tough love. There is no question that you're dealing with a simplistic organism that possesses no ability to reason, but that doesn't mean it won't respond to pain. If, after some extreme encouragement, you still aren't having any luck, I suggest that you adopt. In my experience, I've gotten children to do some pretty impressive things. Think about it.

Amy

Liam Lynch

Dear Liam:

I'm twenty-four and feel like I haven't made the most of my early twenties. What can I do in my mid- to late twenties to make sure I look back on this decade as the best years of my life?

Young but Not That Young

Dear Young but Not That Young:

Don't worry about it. Just live out the rest of your twenties in as boring a manner as you did in your early twenties. Your answer doesn't lie in the present, but in the distant future. It's a time-bending fake perspective you'll start to gain in your thirties. You see, as you get older your life will grow more and more boring, thereby making your twenties seem less boring and more exciting. After you turn forty, you'll look back on your early twenties as the most wild and amazing time of your life. Your memories will mix with your fantasies and dreams. You'll recall all the facts wrong and your shortcomings will end up as tall tales. So cheer up! Your life is only going to get better and better (as you get older and falsely remember your past)!

                                                Liam

                            ...

Dear Liam:
Are you really getting your money's worth at those all-you-can-eat buffets?

                                        Levi K.
                                        Jacksonville, FL

Dear Levi:
I think to answer this question, you need to do some base readings to determine how much is "all you can eat." This is, of course, different for all people based on appetite and stomach capacity. You need to practice this at home first and see how much food you can fit into your body. Also, let's not just define "eating" as chewing and swallowing. Eating actually means "to put food into a body," so even after your stomach is completely full, you can still hold food in your mouth and also insert certain foods into your body anally. Hold as much food in you as possible. When you

have calculated this amount, and the price of the food you were able to hold inside you, then you will know if the buffet price is fair or not.

I think there may also be some sort of legal loophole. You may want to check with the buffet's lawyers but I think that "all you can eat" could possibly mean "all you can eat in your lifetime." "All you can eat" would be from the first thing eaten at birth to your last, dying meal. It could be that a flat price assures you food for the rest of your life, but I'm not certain of this until I look over the buffet contracts.

Liam

...

Dear Liam:

When I ride my bike, I hate jerk-face vehicles that take up the whole road. When I'm driving, I hate jerk-face bicyclists that get in the way. What to do?

Ethan M.

Louisville, KY

Dear Ethan:

You're clearly a man who would benefit from hang gliding. I'm sure it would be extremely easy to build a tower in your yard as a starting point for you to glide over all these people that are causing you so much distress. Please refrain from spitting or throwing things on the many "jerk-faces" below you. Something tells me, though, that you're going to run into some similar problems with jerk-face electrical lines and jerk-face birds.

Liam

. . .

Dear Liam:

My husband doesn't flush the toilet when he poops. Cats can do this, but the thirty-five-year-old man I'm married to can't. How do I train him?

Caroline Larkin

Aurora, CO

Dear Caroline:

You don't train him. This is your first mistake. Like with pets, you need to analyze what your husband is trying to communicate to you. Oftentimes if a cat has an upset stomach or is bleeding in its intestines, it will poop in the bathroom sink. This is because it wants you to take notice that it is not feeling well. Cats also use their poop as a scent marker to claim an area or territory as their own— something like planting a flag and claiming the moon in the name of the United States. When a male human leaves his feces for his mate to look at, it's a clear and simple message: "Look at my awesome poop!"

Liam

...

Dear Liam:

My contact lens is stuck in my eye! It's been in there for like a month now, and I think it's started to meld with my retina. What should I do?!

Corey Morton
Charleston, WV

Dear Corey:

Nothing! Congratulations!! You're an actual cyborg now! Your eye has accepted your correctional lens as an actual part of your body! That's great! Now you don't have to worry about putting contacts in, and buying saline solutions, and remembering to take them out before you go to bed. You have great vision now that your retina is one with your correctional lens. You may want to see if you could upgrade in other ways too. Perhaps your body would consume a hearing aid and improve your hearing tenfold! Perhaps you could ingest a slide whistle into your throat to produce humorous sounds that would amuse your friends. You might want to try to see if your body would meld with a laser pointer inside of your penis. This could be amazing during presentations at work.

Liam

...

Dear Liam:

Lately, my car has been overheating. I opened the Kool-Aid tank and, sure enough, it was out of Kool-Aid, so I put more Kool-Aid in it. It is still overheating! Maybe the thermostat is bad?

> *Alton*
> *Tacoma, WA*

Dear Alton:

Did you check to make sure you don't have a leak in your Yoo-Hoo hose?

> Liam

Simon Rich

Dear Simon:

I have a deep and constant fear of dying in an embarrassing manner. Specifically, being found by firefighters in my underwear. I've seen a psychiatrist about this, but the fear isn't leaving. Do you have any suggestions on how to overcome this fear?

> *Louis*
> *Minneapolis, MN*

Dear Louis:

I'd love to offer you some gentle words of comfort. But as a paid expert, I have no choice but to give you the cold, harsh facts. No matter which precautions you take, it is extremely likely that you will someday be found dead, in your underwear, by firefighters.

According to the National Coroners Society, seven out of

ten deceased Americans are found "By Firemen, in a State of Undress," making it by far the most common form of corpse discovery in the country.

As a resident of Minneapolis, Minnesota, your fear is especially valid. In your hometown, over 90 percent of dead bodies are discovered, unclothed, by firefighters (2012 census, page 3).

In an attempt to assuage your fear, I interviewed your local fire commissioner, Ed Gint. The transcript follows:

SIMON RICH: This scenario—being found dead in one's underwear by firemen—is it really all that common?

FIRE COMMISSIONER GINT: It's so common, we even have a code for it.

SIMON: You do?

FIRE COMMISSIONER: Yeah—Code 1. That's how often it happens.

SIMON: Wow. What's a Code 2?

FIRE COMMISSIONER: "Fire."

SIMON: Let's talk about one of your local residents. Do you happen to know a man named Louis?

FIRE COMMISSIONER: Oh, sure, I see him around. Man... I hope we find that guy dead in his underwear.

SIMON: Really? Why?

FIRE COMMISSIONER: Well...it's not that I want Louis to die. It's just—it would be really funny to find him that way. He has a funny-looking body, silly underwear. It would just be really, really funny.

SIMON: Are you aware that being found dead in his underwear by firefighters is Louis's biggest fear?

FIRE COMMISSIONER: No, I wasn't aware of that.

SIMON: Well, now that you are, will you do me a favor to make Louis feel better? Will you promise that—if you discover Louis's unclothed corpse—you'll treat it with dignity?

FIRE COMMISSIONER: I don't know. I can't really promise that.

SIMON: Why not?

FIRE COMMISSIONER: Well, we're gonna make cracks. He's a funny-looking guy. We're only human.

SIMON: Okay, fair enough. Then how about this: Can you at least promise that you'll try to minimize the number of firemen who are present at his body's discovery? To, say, ten or less?

FIRE COMMISSIONER: I can't promise that.

SIMON: Why not?

FIRE COMMISSIONER: Well, who would I exclude? All of the guys have been looking forward to someday discovering Louis. If it happens, I can't just say, "Half of you stay upstairs—the rest of you, let's have fun."

SIMON: Okay, I guess that makes sense. How about this: Can you at least promise that you won't take any pictures of his half-naked corpse?

FIRE COMMISSIONER: . . .

SIMON: I take it from your silence that you plan on taking pictures.

FIRE COMMISSIONER: Yeah, we're probably gonna take some pictures.

SIMON: All right. What about this: You can take pictures of Louis's half-naked corpse. But will you at least promise not to write any mocking captions underneath the developed prints?

FIRE COMMISSIONER (*long pause*): What counts as mocking?

SIMON: Anything that disparages, say, his level of fatness, or the size of his genitals, or—

FIRE COMMISSIONER: Can't make that promise.

SIMON: Seriously?

FIRE COMMISSIONER: Look, before we sat down, I said I'd be straight with you—so I'm being straight with you.

SIMON: Okay. I appreciate that. Last question: Will you at least promise not to use Louis's naked body as a "prop" for sight gags?

FIRE COMMISSIONER: What counts as a sight gag?

SIMON: Come on, Ed, you know what a sight gag is.

FIRE COMMISSIONER: . . .

SIMON: . . .

FIRE COMMISSIONER: Can't make that promise.

The interview continued for several hours, but you probably don't want to read the rest of it.

In summation, Louis, there's not much you can do to avoid your fate. But I would strongly suggest investing in a pair of long johns.

Sincerely,

Simon Rich

Anne Beatts

Dear Anne:

I'm getting married in a few months and apparently I'm supposed to register for things. Any suggestions?

                                    P. Kuhren
                                    Long Beach, CA

Dear P.:

Since it's impossible to tell by your initial whether you are a man or a woman, I find it difficult to advise you. If, dear P., you are a man, then you can relax because your fiancée will have this covered and you need not do anything, unless of course you are a man marrying a man, in which case you need to rethink your sexual orientation pronto, because a genuine gay man would know this stuff already. If you are a woman and were somehow absent the day they gave out the genes for choosing a china pattern, you should ask your gay friends to help.

Anne

...

Dear Anne:
I'm uninspired, flabby, and alone. How can I jazz up my pathetic existence?

Contemplator of Bloated
Navel
Ottumwa, IA

Dear Contemplator:
First, stop feeling sorry for yourself. Second, cut out all carbs. Third, get out of Ottumwa, Iowa.

Anne

...

Dear Anne:
I'm interested in finding a new job in this shitty economy. Can you advise me which field to look for work in? I am good at nothing.

Kevin Albert
Oshkosh, WI

Dear Kevin:

I would advise you to go into accounting or health care, two sectors which are growing even as the economy is shrinking. Based on the current condition of both our health care and financial systems, you should be fully qualified to succeed in either field. Failing that, you could always become a special advisor to the president.

Anne

. . .

Dear Anne:

How do women wear thongs? They irritate my butt crack and I wind up spending all day trying to pick a wedgie to no avail. I'm starting to think that panty lines are sexy again.

Abby J.

Sandy, UT

Dear Abby:

Used to be, no one's underwear was supposed to show. Then—Madonna. Now bra straps wave freely in the wind, even on bank tellers. So why not visible panty lines? However, if you really want to avoid VPL, you could follow the lead of proto-feminist Germaine Greer and stop wearing underwear altogether. Just avoid being photographed getting out of a limo.

Anne

. . .

Dear Anne:
What are your best tips for living a greener lifestyle?
                              B. Regan
                              Los Angeles, CA

Dear B.:
First, get rid of your car and walk or bicycle everywhere. Second, stop drinking bottled water. Third, raise all your own foodstuffs to reduce the "carbon tax" you pay for having anything shipped to one place from someplace else. (You could make all your own clothes out of hemp, but that's just silly.) Of course, this will necessitate moving away from Los Angeles, but that should be a small price to pay for living green.

You are sincere about this, aren't you? Or do you just want to save the planet as long as it doesn't inconvenience you?
                              Anne

...

Dear Anne:
If you could have one more appendage, what would it do?
                              Christine Yu
                              Oakland, CA

Dear Christine:
It would Tweet for me.
                              Anne

Mike Doughty

Dear Mike:
We're thinking about ordering a pizza, but it just seems like such
a boring, predictable meal. Are we overthinking it?
                                        Shannon and Linda
                                        Atlanta, GA

Dear Shannon and Linda:
There's something about pizza in the South which is really
interesting. You have to do this kind of cognitive discon-
nect from your Grecian ideal of pizza and think about it
more along the lines of bread-item with cheese-and-tomato
stuff, and then it's quite enjoyable. Are you aware of this
practice of putting ranch dressing on pizza? I assure you,
it's everything it sounds like. I was introduced to it by a
travel agent who was hanging out in my motel room. She

had just gotten her belly button pierced and her midsection was wrapped in cellophane. She said her piercer had forbidden her to have sex for a month for sanitary reasons, and I, having taken quite seriously the no-means-no stuff I heard in college in the late eighties, took this as gospel. But in retrospect I think she wanted to sleep with me. In other words, she just wanted some kind of minor stricture to break in the process. Or maybe she wanted me to beg.

Mike

. . .

Dear Mike:
Alcohol is fantastic and sugar is fantastic. Why is sugar alcohol so mean to my digestive system?

Reese
Tom Miner Basin, MT

Dear Reese:
I didn't finish my story about the ranch dressing on the pizza because I was waxing woeful about women who wanted to sleep with me that I was oblivious to. So, I used to order wings along with the pizza just to get the ranch dressing, because I thought it was a special thing the travel agent with cellophane wrapped around her midsection did, and how gruesome, right? But then I realized that I didn't care how the pizza person judged me. I ordered ranch dressing and he added it to the order for an extra seventy-five

cents without batting an eye, and it dawned on me that people actually did this, this was an accepted practice. I wouldn't do it in New York because, though I try to live by the maxim "What other people think of me is none of my business," I don't want to be negatively evaluated, or disdained as a rube.

Mike

. . .

Dear Mike:
My eyeliner keeps smearing underneath my eyes. What's your trick?

David
Eustis, FL

Dear David:
My trick? David, there's no trick! just be honest with yourself! There's no hokum. I promise. And, David, please be happy with yourself just as you are, smearing or no. You know what's been bothering me? Whether Ol' Dirty Bastard was a comedian or not. I mean, many of us judged him as simply crazy, but what was that episode of taking the limo to cash a welfare check on MTV if not genius satire? For a moment, it made me queasy, because I thought maybe I'm a racist for just assuming, as in, "Oh, black guy, must be crazy." But then again, the first time I saw Bobcat Goldthwait not in his eighties character, I was taken aback.

David, I must admit, I still doubt myself. Another remnant from my schooling in those PC-besotted days? Maybe that kind of probing self-doubt about one's attitudes about race should come back, David. I realize the tone of this piece might make you think I mean that in a tongue-in-cheek way, but no, I'm quite serious.

Mike

. . .

Dear Mike:

I've been playing a lot of Cake Mania on my computer lately. I'm disturbed by the number of aliens and sumo wrestlers who come into my fake bakery. Can you think of an explanation for this?

Kelly
Orlando, FL

Dear Kelly:

That's dreadful, but let me finish the thing about ODB: I do this show every year, this benefit, and Chris Rock did it last year—I was out on tour—and I was thinking, if I did it this year, and Chris Rock were to do it again (unlikely, as I was told he had a dreadful time, and was nervous in a way that the organizers I know were extremely tickled to witness), I'd say, "Chris, I have a question for you," and he'd roll his eyes, sigh, another fan, but I'd ask him this question about ODB. And it'd be an honest question, because who else would I know who would've had direct contact with ODB? And it would be a kind of bonding moment with a guy I really feel is a brilliant American poet. Then I feel somewhat guilty for having a scheme like that, in a funny way, as if it were grandiose, but I really just admire the guy, Kelly, you know?

Mike

...

Dear Mike:
I'm uncertain about the intensions [sic] *of my son. He scares me a little. Any thoughts?*

Erin Q.
São Paolo, Brazil

Dear Erin:
Bottom line is: Don't be scared. But I neglected to answer Kelly's question, so let me take a moment to wrap that up: Kelly, if you're still reading, I'm wasting a lot of text-space here, so I should answer succinctly: No, I don't have an explanation for that. In fact, I have to admit, I'm really not much of a games person. Though as a child, I loved my Atari so much, I dreamed of winning a mysterious contest where they'd send me every Atari cartridge that was or would be; I'd have racks, shelves, corridors of cartridges.

I wonder why I lost that? Computer games bore me, and when friends want to hang out and play a board game, I'm like, "Why not just have a conversation? What do we need the game for?" Golf enthusiasts always say, "What a way to get out in the fresh air!" But, Kelly—and Erin, for that matter—can't one just take a walk in the woods? Also, Erin, the way you misspelled intentions as "intensions" is really interesting—a combo of "intense," "intent," and "infusion."

Mike

. . .

Dear Mike:
A coworker consumed a delicious apple I had left on my desk a few days ago. Is it okay for me to steal something of equal value from their desk?

Victor Barkley
Bridgeport, CT

Dear Victor, and David and Reese if you're still reading:
My ex was (uh, is) a playwright, and she wrote a lot of identity politics plays that were actually wickedly funny and brilliant, and subverted the clichés of that form. She even called me a racist once. Actually, it was because I told her a certain part of one of her plays was boring. Seriously, as in, "You don't like that? It's because you're a racist." Stun-

ning. But I took it to heart! At least partially. You know what else she said? She *intended* it to be boring. That just absolutely gob-smacked me. Victor, what the fuck do you say to that? I mean, doesn't that make you want to raise Duchamp from the dead and poke his eyes out with a salad fork?

Mike

Roz Chast

Dear Roz:
I can't seem to get Billy Joel's "Uptown Girl" out of my head. It's been two weeks now. Help!

Adrienne
Boston, MA

Dear Adrienne:
There's only one solution. You have to get another song into your head as soon as possible. Allan Sherman's "Hello Muddah, Hello Faddah" is powerful enough to wipe out almost every other song in existence. Listen to it ten times, and I guarantee you will be praying for "Uptown Girl" to return.

Roz

. . .

Dear Roz:

I have this theory that mustaches only look fetching on firemen. And, for some reason, on dwarves. Who else do mustaches look good on?

> *Graciously,*
> *Penny*
> *West Hartford, CT*

Dear Penny:

It's interesting that you should ask me that. I have tested mustaches of all styles—the "Walrus," the "Toothbrush," the "Lampshade," the "Chevron," the "Fu Manchu," the "Pencil," and many, many more—on both men and women of all ages and sizes. What I have discovered is that mustaches, especially the Fu Manchu, look amazing on babies. If you need evidence, draw a Fu Manchu in permanent marker onto a baby's face and you'll see just what I'm talking about.

> Roz

. . .

Dear Roz:

Ever since I was a little girl I've wanted to become famous. I'm a terrific singer, but success has so far eluded my grasp. I'm now twenty-two. How can I quickly climb my way to the top without alienating friends and family?

> *Ellen*
> *Wahneta, FL*

Dear "Ellen":

First of all, "Ellen," I happen to know that you're not twenty-two. How do I know this? Let's just say I know. "Thirty-eight" is closer to the truth. Also, maybe the reason that success has eluded you is that you're tone-deaf and have no sense of rhythm. Also, "Ellen," I know your so-called "friends and family," and you alienated them a long time ago.

Roz

. . .

Dear *Roz:*

I'm a huge fan of baseball and I love to bring my mitt to professional games just in case an errant fly ball comes my way. Recently, I've been receiving some flak from my wife, who tells me that only children tend to bring mitts to professional baseball games. Where do you stand on this issue?

Scott F.
Lewes, DE

Dear Scott:

Here's what I would do if I were in your shoes: Next time you and your wife go to a baseball game, don't bring your mitt. Dress in business attire, and bring your laptop and a briefcase full of papers. While the ball game is going on, act all busy with your work. Your wife will say, "What are you doing?" and you'll say, "Only children watch the whole baseball game. I'm a busy, busy grown-up!" And she'll say,

"Oh, I see. So you're being Mr. Sarcastic now." And you'll say, "What ever do you mean?" And she'll say, "Don't give me the psychological." Etc. You get the picture.

Roz

...

Dear Roz:

There's a girl in my civics class (I'm in high school) who is extremely shy. I've asked her out a few times, but she just blushes and stammers a response. How can I take it to the next level without appearing too obnoxious or aggressive? I'm kind of shy myself.

Stuart

Dear Stuart:

Do you collect anything that's easily transportable, like old postcards of motel swimming pools or pictures of prison cafeterias? Next time you see her, show her those. They'll work like a charm.

Roz

...

Dear Roz:

I feel like I am smelling the inside of my nose all the time, but the thing is, I don't like the way it smells. How do I fix this?

Chad

Los Angeles, CA

Dear Chad:

I once had something like that happen with the inside of my mouth. It didn't taste bad, but I felt like I couldn't stop tasting it, no matter what I did. I could brush my teeth every five minutes, or eat a box of Oreos. Same deal. I'm sad to say that once you notice this, there is really nothing you can do about it.

Roz

Brendon Small

Dear Brendon:
I'm a full-time carpenter. Is there any chance I might be the Messiah?
> *Blake H.*
> *Tuscaloosa, AL*

Dear Blake:
I've said this a hundred times: Just because you're a smug carpenter who pontificates doesn't make you the Messiah. But then again, you might be. There's only one way to find out: Perform a miracle. Walk on air. Take a running jump off a very high building and walk in place. Write me and let me know what happens. Either way, there is no God.
> Brendon

...

Dear Brendon:
Are the homeless really that well-read?
                                    Jenny Malone
                                    Fairbanks, AK

Dear Jenny:

Maybe you're referencing that movie where Joe Pesci is a homeless genius living in the bowels of Harvard, and Brendan Fraser saves him in some heartwarming way. I'm not sure how the movie ends. A mercy killing? Yes, that's right, a mercy killing. Brendan Fraser kills Joe Pesci's character by suffocating him with a stinky yellowed pillow after Pesci's lobotomy. Great movie!

But to answer your question, I'd say that when it comes to reading the alcohol content on cough syrup bottles, yes: the homeless are incredibly well-read.

                                    Brendon

...

Dear Brendon:
I need a little dental work done. Any suggestions?
                                    Todd Day
                                    Homosassa, FL

Dear Todd:

You will be blown away with what YouTube has to offer in how-to videos. Just type in "molar extraction" and see what pops up. Nine times out of ten, it'll be a college sketch troupe doing yet another commercial parody. But if you sift through the phonies you'll find a watery-eyed lunatic, holding pliers, drunk on bathtub gin, spitting up blood. Watch that and do whatever the guy says.

Brendon

. . .

Dear Brendon:

My girlfriend keeps being the same person, but I want to have sex with different people. Is there any way to make my same girlfriend become a different person when I get tired of having sex with the same person? I'd like to save our relationship.

Tyler Frederickson
Glendale, CA

Dear Tyler:

You've identified the ultimate conundrum: you want the girl but you also want to sleep with others. No man has managed to make this work. Ever. Except for Gene Simmons. He avoided getting married until recently, still has a regular girlfriend, and sleeps with whoever he wants! And he's not even good-looking! How can this be? I'll tell you how it be, Tyler. Gene Simmons is a millionaire.

If you can somehow win millions of dollars (maybe online?) and give it to your girlfriend, I'm nearly convinced that you can create a situation wherein you may sleep with a different lady each night with your girlfriend's consent!

And if for some reason you can't win millions of dollars, don't worry! You can always recede into the impotence of the average miserable American man. Or become a highly skilled crouching masturbator! No big deal!

Brendon

. . .

Dear Brendon:
I was told that at age twenty-seven I will suffer the Saturn return. What is this? Should I be worried?

Ben Patterson
Brooklyn, NY

Dear Ben:
This isn't something to worry about. You just need to return your rental car that day.

Brendon

. . .

Dear Brendon:
My husband and I are trying to teach our teenage children that they don't have to drink to have a good time. The problem is, we

drink to have a good time. Sometimes we drink a lot and have a
really good time! Are we hypocrites?

> Mr. and Mrs. P.
> Madison, WI

Dear Mr. and Mrs. P.:

I appreciate that you're honest about your boozing. The instincts of most parents is to hide alcohol from their children. That's a big no-no. You must train your children how to function while under the influence. Give your children "drunk tests." Send them to school drunk, perhaps on a big test day or when they have to give a book report. Make them get through their flip, silly little child lives totally drunk. Send them to their friends' birthday parties drunk and see if they can keep their shit together! Give them rewards for not acting like drunken assholes!

If your kid can handle these tests, then they will succeed in life where many young celebrities in Hollywood have failed and become the lousy drunks of our world. Make your child the exception. Make your child a good drunk. Make America better. It's up to you, parents. It's up to you.

> Brendon

Cintra Wilson

Dear Cintra:
I'm a nanny for a five-year-old boy and a ten-year-old girl. They still take baths together, which makes me uncomfortable. Should I mention that I think this is a bit inappropriate to their parents?
A Bit Weirded Out
New York, NY

Dear Weirded Out:
I can tell just by the fact that you're a New York nanny that you have never given birth. I think that after you've pushed a naked human out of your own vagina in a cascade of blood and shit, in front of a roomful of people, your whole body-modesty-meter just kind of explodes and never works properly ever again. Not to mention feeding this

little person with your own tits for weeks to months after-ward. I, for one, couldn't convince another friend of mine to put on a shirt for the first three months of her baby's life. It's like, really? . . . If you're not actually using those things, do you really need to be all *National Geographic* right now?

You should try having actual sex every once in a while. If you did, you'd probably slap your forehead and realize that a little girl in the same bathtub as her five-year-old brother is something altogether different. If you told the mom you work for how uptight you are, she'd probably just lay you out with a violent eye roll and start scouring Craigslist for a Brazilian au pair.

Cintra

. . .

Dear Cintra:
I look at myself in the mirror constantly. What is the acceptable amount of times a person can glance at themselves in a reflective sur-face (car, shop window, puddle, etc.) and still be considered modest?

Bob
Austin, TX

Dear Bob:
Oh, so you're a real pretty boy, I guess, huh? Well, Color You Bobra. God. Whatever.

Cintra

. . .

Dear Cintra:

My heart is always open to love and yet I'm single. I have no cats or hobbies other than needlepoint, which is really more of a craft than a hobby. It's an ancient and beautiful tradition that I'm proud to represent in this electronic and digital age. With the fast-moving pace of life, needlepoint grounds me in a way nothing else can. Why am I single?

Bill F.
Hanover, NH

Dear Bill:

Obviously the thing you've set me up to say, right here, is: You're single because you're a needlepoint-doing, bonnet-wearing, Whistler's Mother–type of a guy in a Shaker rocking chair listening to Chanticleer every Tuesday with Morrie, and you can't get laid because your mauve pantaloons are obsessively knotted into a durable woolen grid of double-straight cross-stitches.

If you're going to stick to a postmenopausal art medium like needlepoint, you're going to have to offset the jiggling armpits and wilting flower petals of the whole Yarn Barn ethos with more badass subject matter—like, say, a Bruce Lee poster. Actually, I'd pay a lot of money for a needlepoint Bruce Lee poster. I might even go out with you if you made me one.

Cintra

...

Dear Cintra:
Lately, I find myself watching the birth documentaries on the Life-
time channel just for the sheer joy of seeing the nudity. Has my life
hit rock bottom?

Marc
Rockville, MD

Dear Marc:
I think you should have sex with the nanny who wrote the first
question. Maryland isn't that far from New York. You guys
could always meet in Philadelphia just for the educational
purpose of figuring out what actual sexual-adult-nudity
looks like. Hey, maybe you can invite Bill from New Hamp-
shire to watch, and he can capture the beautiful memory
of you guys fucking in needlepoint. Then you could bring
Bill's badass NC-17 tapestry to Austin, and rub Bob's nose
in it, and say, "See this? This is what actual grown-up inti-
macy looks like. You and the pretty guy reflected in the car
window have a lo-o-o-ong way to go!"

Cintra

...

Dear Cintra:
I've always wanted a nickname, but no one's ever given me one
that's stuck. I'm male, twenty-five, have red hair, and am about

five feet, eight inches tall. I love to bowl and I love to read sci-fi
books. Any suggestions?

> Chris Kastner
> Fanning, MO

Dear Mr. Kastner:

Henceforth, you shall be known as: "The Mexican."

> Cintra

Lisa Lampanelli

Dear Lisa:
I love old suitcases. The kind that are hard and really awkward to travel with. I use them as displays in my house, but if I used them for travel would I go back in time?

Jeannette Windstorm
Linley, KS

Dear Jeannette:
First of all, if I want an old bag that's hard and awkward to travel with, I'll go on vacation with Betty White. And if I want a bunch of old bags lying around, I'll dig up Rue, Bea, and Estelle and stack them in my apartment. I'm sure your cases make wonderful decorative pieces but, with my past banging the brothers, I already have enough baggage in my

life. Oh, and as far as going back in time, I see you live in the middle of freakin' Kansas, so congratulations! Mission accomplished!

Lisa

. . .

Dear Lisa:
Is Jesus a lot of hype?

Artessa Johnson
Seattle, WA

Dear Artessa:
As sure as a name like Artessa signifies you're black, Jesus is without a doubt a lot of hype. First of all, Jesus was believed to be born to a woman who'd never had sex with a man. Puleez! Who does she think she is—Rosie O'Donnell? Then we're supposed to buy that Three Wise Men followed a star to see the King of the Jews. Pushaw! If I wanna meet the King of the Jews, I'll go knock on Seinfeld's front door! And that whole "I am the Messiah" thing. Jesus, please! Jesus said more obnoxious shit than Kanye West! So yeah, much like faux hawks, Silly Bandz, and Lady Gaga, Jesus is just a lot of hype.

Bless you for asking!
Lisa

. . .

Dear Lisa:

When people say they are "chillin' and grillin'," I don't get it. Can you explain this to me?

> *Teddy Bareis*
> *Detroit, MI*

Dear Teddy:

If you add a *g* to the end of each word, this phrase means they are relaxing and preparing a delicious barbecued meal simultaneously. More likely, however, this phrase is being used by painfully square white people, desperately trying to be hip by leaving the *g* off on purpose. Commonly referred to as "wiggers," these people are an embarrassment to both Caucasians and African Americans alike (see Kevin Federline). These douchebags are almost as awful as the breed of folks who use words like "ginormous" and "chillaxin'." Seeing you're from Detroit, Teddy, I realize you don't see a lot of white people, so I don't blame you for being confused by this type of behavior. But, as with the many stray bullets in your city, steer clear when you can. Word to your mother!

> Lisa

. . .

Dear Lisa:

Cesar Millan is a multimillionaire for training dogs? Really? My dog doesn't crap on the carpet and I don't have a TV show

or a three-book deal. How can I parlay my dog's obedience into a
lucrative payday for both of us?

Judd Thompson
Hastings, OK

Dear Judd:

Actually, Judd, Cesar Millan is a multimillionaire from
playing second base for the New York Mets from 1973 to
1977. He is best known for his style of choking way up the
bat and hitting in front of Joe Torre when he set the record
for most double plays grounded into in a single game.
Oh, wait, that was Felix Millan. Sorry. Actually, I have no
freakin' clue who Cesar Millan is!

But since your name is Judd and it's not followed by
Apatow AND you live in Oklahoma, I'm guessing you
live in a trailer with your sister/wife and you've built either
a still, meth lab, or both in your bathroom. Therefore, I
imagine a lucrative payday for you is probably just enough
to buy a fifth of Absolut and a pack of unfiltered Camels.
So sell your mangy pup and get to the liquor store before it
closes! Hope that helps!!

Lisa

. . .

Dear Lisa:

My cousins are racist. How can I make them like me without enabling their bigotry?

Thanks,
Greg

Dear Greg:

You didn't include what city you live in but I'm gonna guess it's Politically-Correctsville, U.S.A. You're the kind of phony liberal who calls black people "African Americans" and Asian people "Yellow Americans," and this BS keeps bigotry alive in this country. You give power to so-called "racist" words by avoiding them. Come on, just for once say the n-word. And resist the urge to leave off the "er." Come on, say it! Too much for you? Okay—at least try "Spook." That could mean a ghost or goblin. Very good! Now try "Gook." Why? Because it's hilarious and it even rhymes, just like "Spic" and "Mic." Hysterical! Be honest, Greg—don't you feel better already? Now go play nice with your kinfolk, y'hear?

Lisa

...

Dear Lisa:

When did chocolate get so fancy? What the hell is wrong with a good ol' Hershey's bar?

Midge Edgington
Biloxi, MS

Dear Midge:

You are absolutely correct! Chocolate has gotten too damned highfalutin! If I want chocolate-covered nuts, I'll drip Bosco onto my husband's ball sack! And if I want a chocolate-covered cherry, I'll dip my vag in a fondue pot.

To answer your question, this disturbing occurrence happened around the same time coffee got hoity-toity and phones became a hot topic of conversation. If I'm within earshot of you ordering a Venti Vanilla Soy Decaf Latte, prepare to have it spilled in your lap like that dumb cunt who burnt her cooch up with McDonald's coffee 'cause she didn't realize it was HOT! And if I'm at a party and you start telling me about the latest app you just downloaded for your brand-new Droid, pray you have an app for extracting the phone from your anus. So, Midge, have a good ol' Hershey's bar on me, and if you'd like to learn more about chocolate, buy my newest tome, *Chocolate, Please: My Adventures in Food, Fat and Freaks.* (How's that for a shameless Jew plug?!?)

Lisa

...

Dear Lisa:
Would I be a better person, or at least healthier, if I were grass-fed?
Matt Ostasiewski
Salt Lake City, UT

Dear Matt:

Yes, my Mormon friend, being grass-fed will make you a healthier and better person (although cows are grass-fed and look how fat and disgusting they are). You see, Matt, meat these days—much like A-Rod, Andy Pettitte, and Roger Clemens—is loaded with hormones and growth-promoting additives. Studies show that grass-fed animals lead low-stress lives and are so healthy there's no need to pump them full of drugs like Lindsay Lohan on a Saturday night. Plus your wife or, in your case, WIVES will be much happier since a grass-fed diet will make your "beef" much more tender and succulent. Bon appétit!

Lisa

Alan Zweibel

Dear Alan:
Seriously, what is Cher eating or drinking to keep her looking exactly the same as when she shook her ass on that navy boat?

Shauna Bonham
Sacramento, CA

Dear Shauna:

Sorry, but I have no idea which navy boat you're referring to, as the iconic singer-actress has had a curious propensity for showing up unannounced and shaking her ass on the decks of battleships ever since her divorce from the late Sonny Bono in 1975. (Last March, she surprised the crew of the USS *Nimitz* at a pre-reveille hour with an ass-shaking rendition of "Half Breed.") But the ass-shaking occasion most folks remember took place in 1989 aboard the USS *Missouri* when she sang "If I Could Turn Back Time" wearing a fishnet body stocking under a very revealing black bathing suit. Cher looks sexy and fit in that video, and the singer-actress, now eighty-four, still looks just as good thanks to a special diet that has her eating footage of that very video three times a day.

Alan

...

Dear Alan:

I'm only twenty-six and I'm already going gray. Is this something I should be worried about? Am I aging at an accelerated rate?

Brian Searle
Bellingham, WA

Dear Brian:

Yes, this is something you should worry about! However, I strongly advise against doing so, as worrying could very well make your hair grayer. But even if you're indeed aging at an accelerated rate, fret not. Remarkable strides are being made in gerontology with new drugs and treatment plans a mere two years away. So help is on the way for you, Brian—unless, of course, you die of old age before then.

Alan

...

Dear Alan:
In the Mark Twain autobiography that was just published, there are some remarkable and (I think) false claims. But with him being dead, we can't very well dispute him. Or can we?

> *Artie Lefkowitz*
> *Tucson, AZ*

Dear Artie:
I totally understand why you'd question the veracity of someone who releases his autobiography a hundred years after his death. At the very least, his memory would be a tad fuzzy, so details run the possibility of not being precise. But in this case, why not cut him a little slack and let it go? The guy wrote *Huckleberry Finn,* for god's sake.

> Alan

...

Dear Alan:
My boyfriend is a mascot for our college team (Go Panthers!) and his antics are wildly popular. After a game he's on top of the world and will sometimes stay in costume for a good two days, but as soon as that giant head comes off he becomes moody and distant, and sometimes sobs uncontrollably. Should he just wear it all the time? That can't be healthy, right?

> *Ted*
> *Chama, NM*

Dear Ted:

While some maintain it's abnormal that a young man functions best when inside the body of a large fake cat, history tells us he's in excellent company, as Albert Einstein himself figured out ($E = MC^2$) while prancing across the Princeton campus dressed as their mascot (Go Tigers!). A year later, when he removed the tiger head to accept his Nobel Prize, Albert wailed like a banshee until he put the head back on and then proceeded to skip through the streets of Stockholm chanting, "I won! I'm smart! I'm very, very smart!"

Alan

. . .

Dear Alan:

Could it be remotely possible that the voices I hear softly singing as I walk among the wildflowers belong to angels?

Julie W.
Alden, IA

Dear Julie:

It depends on what songs we're talking about. Since angels hate rap and country music, if it's Snoop Dogg and Merle Haggard you're hearing, there's a greater chance that Snoop and Merle themselves are squatting and singing in those wildflowers. And contrary to popular belief, angels absolutely detest hymns. But if it's Eydie Gormé's "Blame It on the Bossa Nova" you hear . . . yep, that's them.

Alan

Julie Klausner

Hi Anonymous:

First of all, don't you love that expression: "Awk-ward!"? I certainly do. I also like "Tell us how you really feel" and "That's gonna leave a mark!" That second one is a thing you say while somebody near you is hurt physically, and instead of running to their defense, you're like, "I'm going to stand here and say something I stole from that old lady with the craggy face and saggy breasts from the Shoebox

Greetings birthday cards." And when the cops come and give you a look like, "This woman is bleeding internally and you just stood there and said something about leaving a mark," you twiddle your thumbs (or breasts) and you're like, "Awk-ward!"

So, to answer your rather McMahononian question, "How awkward is it?" as pertaining to your attractive "OMG-YN": In all honesty, it does sound pretty awkward.

But that's not to say you should be pounding the Cigna directory for a suitably repellent alternative to *Dr. T. & the Women* starring Richard Gere. It just depends on how comfortable you are flirting with somebody whose job it is to make sure your ovaries don't wither, or your cervix doesn't turn to clay, or that your various O'Keeffeian plumbing doesn't malfunction in a disgusting or upsetting manner.

If you're afraid of being honest about what ails you in the pants at the risk of seeming coy or dumb or however it is ladies like to act these days to make it so men want to get their John Hancocks all tangled up in their corn mazery, then you owe it to your tubes and their surrounding garden furniture to seek gynecological assistance elsewhere.

And if you're like, "Fuck it, my pussy is my best feature," then Godspeed, Anonymous. Go forth, and make things awkward like a fox.

Julie

. . .

Dear Julie:
Is it okay to enjoy blackface if you're doing it ironically?
                                        Arabella H.
                                        Brooklyn, NY

Look, Arabella:
It's one thing if you're asking about taking in a quiet evening of minstrelsy, maybe with a glass of Peen-Greege and some YouTube Heckle and Jeckle. That brings along with it a discussion of context, and all the Proustian whatnots about seeing *Dumbo* with your dad as a little girl and how you thought those crows shucking and jiving were funny then, because you were six, and how were you to know that one day Spike Lee would make *Bamboozled* and then later *She Hate Me*. But the most important thing to learn about blackface in terms of the cultural history of it is that it's just that: history. Irony or shmirony, blackface is something that, today, you should never do.

Unless you love to laugh.

                                        Julie

···

Dear Julie:
I think my cat is starting to get complacent. How do I put a little fear of God into him and let him know there's no such thing as a free lunch?
                                        Jeanna
                                        Northern Florida

Dear Jeanna:

It's a testament to the power of two clichés in a row that if it weren't for the first sentence of your letter, I'd think you were not crazy. But you are, so let's go to it.

How does one teach status to a cat? They are not, after all, pack animals cognizant of alphas and betas and other kinds of Greek marshmallow-based cereal. But they do understand the hanky code of yore. Are you familiar? It's a thing where gay dudes would put different colored handkerchiefs in the pockets of their leather sport jackets in hopes of attracting men they would, decades later, still be unable to marry.

White was meant to indicate an interest in mutual masturbation. Red: anal fisting. And unless you have the flexibility of a Bikram yoga instructor and no hang-ups about urine or snakes, you do not even want to know what a polka-dotted hanky meant.

As far as your cat is concerned, I think you should go to the fabric store and buy a bunch of swatches. Wear a new piece of fabric like a hanky around him or her (always her) every day. Soon enough, that snotty cat will be God-fearing and even might start paying for lunch. With Cat Money!

Julie

...

Dear Julie:

I got a black eye after falling down some stairs. Seriously. But every time I explain that to my friends, they assume I'm covering up an *abusive relationship. How do I make it obvious that my boyfriend isn't smacking me around and I honestly am just a clumsy ass?*

Two Left Feet in Kentucky

Dear Lefty:

Have you ever considered having an affair with somebody who is abusive? That way you wouldn't be lying to your friends, who seem nice. Also, what kind of stairs give you a black eye? Constantly turning Busby Berkeley stairs? If that is your case, I suggest you invest in a case of Max Factor foundation, or whatever those thirties chorus girls must have used to cover up their Berkeley-given shiners. Also, while you're at it, you may as well give your hair a pin curl, lower the hem of your skirt, and tweeze your eyebrows into oblivion. Your new look is likely to allure one of your suitors and enrage the other. Remember, because now you have an abusive lover? Get to juggling suitors, young lady, and the respective lovemaking and domestic violence that comes along with the task at hand!

Julie

...

Dear Julie:

My mother says that nobody has good manners anymore. This coming from a woman who fucked three strangers at Woodstock. Does her moral grandstanding carry any weight at all?

S. Petrova

Memphis, TN

Dear Señor Petrova:

Wow! Really? Only three? Good for her for exercising the sixties version of portion control in what I'm certain must have been a tempting situation. Wait, unless you're talking about "Woodstock '94." Do you remember that? And how it was sponsored by a northeastern home electronics chain called Nobody Beats the Wiz? We all thought that was so funny, because the original Woodstock did beat the Wiz, or maybe I don't really understand what "funny" means.

The point is that Woodstock '94 had a little more mud than the original Woodstock, and there was way more Aphex Twin. So if your mom fucked some strangers in the mid-90s, I can't help you. That is disgusting.

But if you're saying what I think you are, about the original lineup and Sha Na Na and all of it, then who are we to tell ourselves our parents are something more or less than people? And people are fallible, braless, brown-acid-imbibing filth sluts sometimes. It has been proven by science!

So, listen to Mrs. Manners-Petrova when she reminds you not to slurp your soup. At worst, it could be malarkey, and at best, it could be a revolting euphemism for a sexual act she endured in the company of at least two members of the Spin Doctors. Oh, wait. Did I forget what "worst" and "best" mean again?

Julie

. . .

Dear Julie:

Is it creepy to plan your own funeral? I'm not sick and I don't intend on dying anytime soon, but when the time comes, I don't want my family, who managed to ruin my wedding, to screw up my "other" big day. Is this selfish?

> *Planning Ahead*
> *Sacramento, CA*

Dear Planning Ahead-ache is more like it:

Wow! You seem like a really fun, "California" type of person. You collect grudges, you're super into "own-funeral-planning," and you're the human equivalent of an avocado or a Mike Love vocal break!

My advice for you is to go about doing exactly what you've been doing, only maybe intend on dying soon a little more. And please write back and tell me how your family ruined your wedding.

Seriously, I'm curious! Did they try to jump out of the cake? They can't do that with a real cake! It ruins the cake, and also, as a side note, I hate it when more than one person jumps out of a cake. I've never seen it but I'm pretty sure I'd hate it. It's a cake, not a clown car! Unless it's one of those cakes they make especially for clowns on that *Ace of Cakes* show. But if a clown was going to get a cake, do you really think he'd want one in the shape of a car? He probably wouldn't. Hey, look at me: I know what clowns think!

> Julie

. . .

Dear Julie:

I've been seeing this very attractive, smart, sweet, nice guy for a while now. What's the problem? He's not funny. Not even a little bit. The text message one-liners are little suicides. And the worn-down observational humor gives me crushing genital sadness.

Tell me what to do before I commit a serious crime against an otherwise wonderful human being.

Sophia Devareaux

Dear Sophia:

Give me twenty-four hours, and I will marry you off to a clown.

Julie

Rich Fulcher

Dear Rich:

My boyfriend wants to know how many guys I've been with before him. I'm worried that the number might be a little too high. What's the etiquette on this? Should I tell him the truth, or what he wants to hear?

Susan B.
Rochester, NY

Dear Susan:

Your boyfriend asked you how many guys you've slept with and then you left the room to write me this letter? Is he still waiting? He probably thinks the number is so huge that you need one of those military mainframe computers from *I Dream of Jeannie* to figure it out. Talk about bad etiquette!

There's no way out of this now except to go right back

in and ignore him. Pretend you forgot because you were distracted with your coin collection: "Honey, I'm sorry, the 1970 uncirculated Kennedy half-dollars have been oxidized. What was your question again? Ah, yes. I've only slept with three guys."

Rich

...

Dear Rich:

I just found out that I'm pregnant and I think it might be a good idea to give up the baby. But now my mom wants to adopt it. If this kid comes into our home, what's my technical relationship to it? Let's say it's a girl—does it count as my daughter or my younger sister? And who's responsible for buying diapers?

Confused Mom-to-Be

Berkeley, CA

Dear Confused:

This question had me so bewildered that I was nearly ready for a procrastinatory masturbation session until I read you were from Berkeley. It all makes sense now. Your mom is probably part of some radical underground organization like the Weather Department or Green Post. She probably put you on the Pill when you were nine just so she could adopt your child and win brownie points with the growingly suspect neighbors, who constantly object to your Eldridge Cleaver holiday wreath.

If you have any decency you will send this baby to Kansas, where the only time she hears the word Mao is when she's downing an all-American bison burger with a side of liberty rings.

Rich

P.S. I've recently been informed that the Pill actually stops you from getting pregnant, so . . . go buy those Huggies for your sister.

. . .

Dear Rich:
I've always thought that polyester is kinda sleazy. So why do old people wear it so often? Are they being ironic?

S.J.
Savannah, GA

Dear S.J.:
You could not be more wrong(er). Polyester is a secret garment worn by the Old Guard protectors of Gorthrab, King of the Slug Charmers (See: Twelfth Century). In order to wear this coveted garment, one must go through 17 Ladders of Assessment, including Chop the Dishtowel, Seek the Elderberry, and Advanced Parallel Parking. Each of these tasks take years of preparation and can only be administered on a Leap Day (see: *Groundhog Day*—it's a great movie).

Rich

...

Dear Rich:

I left my family's Easter celebrations early because I ate too much candy and got sick, but everyone thinks I faked it because I hate them. How can I win back their affection?

Finn P.

Salem, OR

Dear Finn P.:

You are fucked. If you "win" back their affection by being nice, then they know you lied. The only option is to get sick every time you meet them. I suggest swallowing some kind of turd. Other things may make you sick but I can't think of any offhand. In order to make your contention believable, I suggest you make yourself ill at the next fourteen family gatherings. Bon appétit!

Rich

...

Dear Rich:

I heard that diet drinks cause cellulite. I don't like using Google so could you just tell me if it's true or what?

Jennifer B.

Ogden, UT

Dearest Jennifer:
I'm afraid diet drinks don't cause cellulite; they cause serious red mite infestation. Please remove all loose bedding and burn your property.

Rich

. . .

Dear Rich:
I have always been curious as to why there is no better culinary term for "meatball." Any ideas?

Rob DeSue

Dear Rob and Sue:
You are so funny. Do you like to go see comedy at the clubs? Me too. I don't just want it to be a crapshoot, though, and wind up spending twenty-five bucks to see Joe Schmoe from Palookatown. That's why I'll pay a little bit extra to see a Dane Cook or a Carlos Mencia when I know I'll get a real corker of a good night. Do you like Parcheesi? I sometimes swim in wine.

Rich

. . .

Dear Rich:
My wife and I want to experiment with S&M, but we're unclear on the rules. How do you decide who gets to be the dominant one

and who has to wear the handcuffs and have things done to his or
her nipples? Should we flip a coin?

Anonymous
Chicago, IL

Dear Anonymous:

Are you sure you're not my congressman who I saw at that
"Eyes Wide Shut Party" about two years ago? Remember?
I believe you spilled cider on my harness and kept brag-
ging to me that you had a split dick and your wife was
into space docking. Anyway, I really admire your stand on
illegal immigration.

Rich

Merrill Markoe

Dear Merrill:

Say you've discovered you have bedbugs—at what point do you have to tell your roommates? And say those roommates are not actually your roommates, but a girl who just spent the night and is now asking what all the "red marks" are on her arms. What then?

Sammy
St. Paul, MN

Dear Sammy:

In a situation this dicey, obviously you should put off any discussion as long as you can. After that, I recommend a two-part program:

1. Begin by telling her, with a certain amount of awe, that red marks on the arms are a well-known side effect of a multiorgasmic sexual experience. This almost definitely

will guarantee you a follow-up date. But if by then you have so many bugs that the mattress seems to be vibrating on its own, explain that the shimmy is an illusion caused by the incredible sexual energy generated between the two of you.

2. When this stops working (and it will), there's nothing left for you to do to counter her rage except to be proactive. Begin by calling her a frigid slut who is so locked into an airtight middle-class shell of comfort that she will never experience a meaningful life. Then, as you throw her out, insist that you never had any trouble with bedbugs until she started spending the night. Remember to add, before you slam the door shut, that since she is spreading an infestation, she is morally obligated to inform all the other guys she is fucking. Now go buy your friends a pitcher of beer and celebrate yet another win-win situation for Sammy from St. Paul.

Merrill

...

Dear Merrill:

My mom believes in UFOs. How long should I wait before I introduce new girlfriends to her?

Greg

St. Louis, MO

Dear Greg:

Well, it's never wise to introduce a mom to a new girlfriend before the six-month mark—it's only then that things will have begun to get serious enough to either merit a mom encounter or to come apart for unavoidable reasons. Having cleared that hurdle, next I suggest that you check with your mom's psychic, astrologer, and numerologist for a comprehensive list of the times most compatible with her current UFO schedules. Input the data into your computer and collate them onto a spreadsheet that will offer a clear path to the best dates for the introduction. But I might as well warn you that no matter how much careful work you put into the architecture of the whole matter, there remains an almost 100 percent chance that your mom isn't going to like your new girlfriend anyway. That's just the way it works with moms and new girlfriends, as any good feng shui practitioner or aromatherapy expert will tell you.

Merrill

. . .

Dear Merrill:
My wife is depressed and crying all the time. How do I cheer her up?

Anonymous

Dear Anonymous:
There is only one way to cheer up a depressive . . . and that is to present yourself as more depressed than they are. So begin right now by collecting a stack of hideous international news reports, crime scene accounts, and scientific papers detailing the threat of epidemics and world calamities.

Before asking your wife what in particular is bothering her, select the stories that will easily beat hers in a one-on-one contest. And then when she begins to list her problems, go ahead and top her. For added fun, assign points for relative misery. If she says, "I am fat and no one loves me anymore," shout out: "Okay! That's fifty points for you!" Then read an article out loud written by someone who spent his childhood running from the Janjaweed militia. This should nab you an easy five thousand points in a single clip.

Having successfully eliminated your wife from the competition, remember to be a gracious winner and offer her a nice cup of hot chocolate and a piece of pie before you ask her if she is ready to go another round. This is only fair.

Merrill

Fred Willard

Dear Fred:
Do you believe in UFOs? Have you ever been captured? If so, what happened?

> *Robert F.*
> *Greenwood, MS*

Dear Robert:
Why, yes, I was captured and probed and prodded in every part and crevice of my body. But it later turned out they were not aliens, so the joke was on me. As a result, the whole UFO question is still, unfortunately, "up in the air."

> Fred

. . .

Dear Fred:

I'm thirty-five years old and, because of a financial situation (I've been unemployed since 2008), have had to move in with my elderly parents. Should I even tell the women I'm dating that I'm living at home? Should I be honest or lie? I'm embarrassed, quite frankly.

Tony
Brookridge, VT

Dear Tony:

Simply tell the women it's your house, and the older people upstairs are merely working on a TV series of *Psycho.*

Fred

. . .

Dear Fred:

I was just invited to a cuddle party and would love to know what is an appropriate gift for the host. Any advice? Brownies? Something else freshly baked? This is not a joke. And, yes, this is my first cuddle party.

Marcy St. John

Dear Marcy:

You never go into a "cuddle party" unprepared. Contact me and we'll run a whole workshop of "cuddle" exercises, including improv, sense memory, exploration, and the very important "Yes...and" response game. As for a gift, the only one you should bring is the gift of "shhh."

Fred

. . .

Dear Fred:
My husband wants to take an expedition into the Amazon forest—
by himself! He got this idea watching a documentary on the Dis-
covery Channel. Should I persuade him otherwise? I'm nervous,
but don't want to damage his fragile male psyche. Any advice?

Brenda
Reading, PA

Dear Brenda:
Your husband is hoping you'll object and talk him out
of it. But tell him he's a hero, make sure his insurance is
up-to-date, send him off with a worried look, and sit back
and enjoy the best vacation of your life.

Fred

. . .

Dear Fred:
I am getting married next spring to a man with a twenty-one-
year-old daughter. She wants to be the ring bearer. Am I being
mean to think that she's too old for such a role?

Anonymous

Dear Anonymous (if that really is your fake name):
There's no such thing as "too old." Welcome her and make
sure you're seen laughing and frolicking with her at the recep-
tion. It'll make you seem really young.

Fred

...

Dear Fred:
I'm still at a loss as to what a "key grip" does on a film stage.
Anything important?

> Ben Mathews
> Ft. Lauderdale, FL

Dear Ben:
He's the head light man on the set. The crew's main job is
to play poker and swap dirty stories with the leading lady,
so she doesn't seem "standoffish" and so that she can tell
people she was just "one of the guys." Please contact me
for a description of "best boy," as well as the differences
between producer, executive producer, assistant producer,
associate producer, and supervising producer.

> Fred

...

Dear Fred:
My roommate is a total slob and I can't stand it any longer. To
give you an example, she leaves toenail clippings throughout the
apartment's floor and every night she leaves the sink filled with
dishes. She also has a terrible temper and I'm afraid to confront
her directly. What would you do in my situation?

> Kirsten D.
> Skidmore, MO

Dear Kirsten:

Try to find out why she is so terrible tempered. Sit down with her and tell her you'll gladly do more of the chores and happily— Oh, wait a minute. Why not just move out?

Fred

Miscellaneous Canadian Rock Musicians

Dear John K. Samson of The Weakerthans:
Whenever I try baking cookies, the batter always comes out too
runny. Am I using too much milk or not enough powdered sugar?
Also, I suspect that my wife may be cheating on me. How can I
trap the deceitful bitch in her own web of lies?

Confused in Portland

Dear Confused:
Why is everyone suddenly using the word "bitch"? It is
creepy. Recently I was on a snorkeling boat in the South
Pacific, watching snorkelers snorkel (as I am mildly afraid
of the water) with another snorkeling abstainer, a kind
woman from New Jersey. She told me about how, before her
vacation, she had taken a course to try to cure her full-on

aquaphobia. They asked participants to put their faces in a bowl of water, and she couldn't even bring herself to try. I looked around at the miles of choppy open ocean and tried to move the conversation toward something that would distract her from the fact that she was surrounded by her greatest fear. I asked what she thought of the upcoming U.S. presidential race and she said she liked Obama but thought he was inexperienced, and loved Bill Clinton but thought Hillary was "kind of a bitch." I didn't know how to respond to any of that, and then her husband swam up to the boat, spat some water through his snorkel, and yelled, "Get in the water! Right now!" I bet you are like him, and deserve some misfortune—a good cuckolding or shark attack. Try granulated sugar instead of powdered.

John K. Samson

...

Dear Owen Pallett of Final Fantasy:
Are babies worth the hassle of pregnancy?

An Unwilling Mother
Jacksonville, FL

Dear Unwilling Mother:
This is an excellent question. I don't have any children, nor am I a woman, so I went to an expert: my mother. She said, "No. The nine months of pregnancy are just the beginning. Once the baby is born, you will lose your identity. Your baby's birth will also be your death. Not literally, of course,

but the death of the vibrant, exciting woman that you've spent your whole life working on. You will lose contact with friends. Your writing will suffer. And the so-called "bliss of parenthood" is a sham, too. You'll find yourself talking less about your beautiful new infant and more about the weight you've gained."

Thanks, Mom! I love you too.

Owen Pallett

. . .

Dear Steve Bays of Hot Hot Heat:
I'm getting married next winter, and I'm already concerned about the ceremony. My family is Jewish, my fiancé's family is Catholic, and he's an agnostic. Is there a way for the wedding to combine all of our beliefs without offending anybody?

Anxious Bride
St. Louis, MO

Dear Anxious Bride:
When my good friend Tobias, a practicing Muslim, and his fiancée, Shauntrice, an orthodox Jew, were to be wed, Shauntrice's Wiccan parents refused to attend if Tobias's casual Afro-Caribbean voodoo-practicing family were to be present. Notably distraught over this pickle, I suggested to Tobias that he simply hold his wedding in a square, windowless, concrete storage facility and divide the building into four sections with yellow police tape. The couple

would then recite their vows cross-legged, each with a leg in one of the four sections. The "minister" of sorts—ordained through an anonymous religion-neutral Internet site—would be lowered from the ceiling and hover over the couple and all four families. Long story short, the wedding went off without a hitch and, although now divorced, the couple couldn't have been happier with my basic, common-sense suggestions for their special day.

Steve Bays

...

Dear A. C. Newman of The New Pornographers:
I'm much better at cooking than baking. I've heard that people who excel at cooking are right-brained while bakers tend to be left-brained. Could this be true?

Desperate in the Kitchen
San Francisco, CA

Dear Desperate:
As far as I know, baking is the same as cooking, isn't it? Isn't baking a form of cooking? Am I alone on this one? This is a trick question. There is no logical answer. Who put you up to this? Was it my wife? You know, I don't cook because I *can't* cook. It is not laziness. Is the world a better place if I fill it with my shitty cooking?

A. C. Newman

...

Dear Steven Page, formerly of the Barenaked Ladies:
All my friends are having babies, so I bought a puppy. Whenever they
start talking about baby stuff, I talk about my dog. But they usually
glare at me like I'm an idiot. Do I need new friends or a baby?
                              Allison

Dear Allison:

I think you need to stop speaking with these "friends." You
do not have enough in common. For example, you seem to
think that having a dog is somehow equivalent to having an
actual human child. You obviously have no idea what it's like
to have a child. I wonder if you ever were a child. Did you
feel like a dog when you were a child? Do you think that the
three-year-old Allison was somehow intellectually or emotion-
ally equivalent to a three-and-a-half-month-old dog? (I cling
fast to the dog-year conversion laws.) I think your problem is
not with your friends, but in how little you actually respect
yourself, for which those of us with children have no time.

                              Steven Page

...

Dear Sara Quin of Tegan and Sara:
My little brother said we should smoke some weed together, but I
don't want him taking pictures and blackmailing me with them.

Should I address this to him directly or is there a way I can get around it without bringing it up at all?

Dale Shipley
Naples, FL

Dear Dale:

It's a trap. My older sister publicly resolved to discontinue her addiction to nicotine at midnight on January 1, 2007. She declared her abstinence from the dirty habit and promised, in a binding agreement with a friend, to pay one thousand dollars to anyone who caught her inhaling. At 3:23 a.m. on January 1, 2007, my sister arrived home from the bar, under the influence of alcohol, and disturbed my slumber by blasting songs from her electro-pop side project while dancing around the inflatable mattress I was sleeping on in her living room. She then proceeded to smoke her face off while mocking my good behavior. I quickly turned on my video camera and captured her in the act. I then used the incriminating tape to receive my thousand-dollar reward. I also called her "watpagin" for three months following a predictive text mishap from the same evening. Don't ever trust a sibling not to sell you out for laughs or money.

Sara Quin

Elizabeth Beckwith

Dear Elizabeth:

I'm a world-class thumb wrestler. I win every time. My boyfriend gets so frustrated when he loses against me that he slinks around with his head hung the whole day. Do I throw a fight to make him feel better?

> *Barb O'Conner*
> *San Antonio, TX*

Dear Barb:

Sorry, Barb, I am calling bullshit on your self-proclaimed "world-class" thumb wrestler status. Anyone who knows anything about professional thumb wrestling knows that there is only one person who has ever held that title, and his name was not Barb O'Conner. Does the name Hal "Hitch Hiker" Hudson mean anything to you? Or am I mistaken and you invented the Flying Metacarpal Crusher? I resent that you assume I am such a novice to the world of thumb wrestling that I would fall for your ruse. I grew up in Las Vegas, Barb. There wasn't an International Thumb Wrestling Federation tournament that I did not attend as a child. My bedroom walls were covered in photos of such luminaries as Robby "Knuckles" Jackson, Tiffany "Toe Thumbs" Taylor, and Sylvia "Three Joints" Cortez. You insult my intelligence, Barb. Oh, and FYI, "throwing a fight" would keep you out of the Thumb Wrestling Hall of Fame, but I assume you know that since you are a "world-class" thumb wrestler and all. The audacity!

Elizabeth

. . .

Dear Elizabeth:
I hate working. Is there any way I can get out of this horrible,
imposed social contract?

R. Penn
Charleston, SC

Dear R. Penn:
My gut tells me that you are a lazy bastard who has never worked a hard day in his life. Am I wrong? Look at you, you couldn't even muster the energy to write your entire first name. I don't even know if you are a man or a woman. But what do you care, "R"? You only care about yourself and your desire to avoid any sort of labor. You disgust me.

Perhaps if you spent the energy that you exerted avoiding work, you could have accomplished something other than writing a desperate letter to an expert like myself.

Nice, "R." You think I don't know that you are making a rude face at me right now? What? You think that just because my job consists of sitting around drinking coffee and coming up with "zingers" that I don't have a "real job"? I resent that you are insinuating that, "R." No, I'm not getting defensive, "R," you're getting defensive. All right, you know what, let's just both calm down for a minute.

It's funny, "R," when I started this letter I really hated you, but you're kind of turning me around here. You can be very persuasive when you want to be. That's a gift, "R," that's a real gift. Perhaps I misjudged you.

To answer your question, I don't think you can avoid working, nor should you. Not when you have this tremendous gift that I am, admittedly, just now recognizing. I pray that you find a job that you love and a career worthy of your talents. Good luck!

Elizabeth

. . .

Dear Elizabeth:
I suspect that my allergies are all in my head. How can I overcome them?

Jonathon Holtzman
Seattle, WA

Dear Jonathon:

Have you considered hypnosis? It is lucky that you contacted me—I happen to be somewhat of a hypnosis expert. And by "expert" I mean that I have watched endless repeats of every episode of every sitcom in which a character is hypnotized. I'm going to need you to relax, Jonathon. Now, clear your mind of everything but the image of your allergies vanishing and count backward from ten to one. You are getting very sleepy, Jonathon, very sleepy. When you awaken your allergies will be gone forever, but you will also think you are a chicken for no reason, clucking anytime someone says the word "spaghetti." Additionally, you will realize that Elizabeth Beckwith is the most brilliant, original person you have ever come across in the whole wide world ever, ever, and you will tell others of your mind-blowing discovery. You and your ragtag group of friends known as "Beckwithians" will go door-to-door spreading the news of your new hero, the most amazing person in the world, Elizabeth Beckwith.

Humbly yours,

Elizabeth

P.S. Spaghetti.

...

Dear Elizabeth:

My girlfriend is getting fat. I still love her, and I'll keep loving her even if she keeps getting fatter, but I liked it more when she wasn't.

*Fat, that is. How do I tell her to stop getting fat without hurting
her feelings/her breaking up with me?*

Name withheld

Dear Name withheld:

Oh my gosh, you are just the sweetest. The fact that you
would continue to love your girlfriend even after she got
fat, and even if she continues to get fatter, makes you the
most wonderful person I have ever heard of. Wow! Why
would anyone ever break up with you, the most loving,
open-minded, least shallow person in the whole wide world?
I mean, do you hear yourself? You are willing to love a person even after they got very fat. I live in Los Angeles, and I
can say, with complete authority, I have never heard of such
a thing. I think if you tell your girlfriend that you would
prefer that she not get any fatter, she will wrap you up in
the biggest hug you have ever experienced and tell you, "No
problem, sweetheart. I will do whatever it takes to keep you
happy because, after all, you are a one-in-a-million person
and your happiness is my priority." She would be crazy to
get upset and risk losing you. You have nothing to be afraid
of. Trust me, women don't mind being called fat if it is by
someone like you. My list of the most selfless people who
have ever existed is as follows: 1) Jesus 2) Gandhi 3) Name
withheld.

Elizabeth

. . .

Dear Elizabeth:

I asked a girl to marry me. She said no. Now we're dating again. Can I use the same ring to propose again if I put it in a different box?

> Nick Brignola
> Easton, PA

Dear Nick:

I feel awkward saying what I am about to say to you in a public forum but you leave me no choice. We are not dating again. We were never dating to begin with. You bought me one cup of coffee nine years ago when I met you at that coffee shop while passing through Pennsylvania. The first time you proposed to me I was flattered, if more than a little shocked. Please do not propose to me again, Nick. I am already married to someone that I love very much. I know this is difficult for you to accept, and you contacting me in this way makes me suspect that you are off your meds again. I wish you all the best, but please do not contact me ever again. Let me say this as clearly as I can: Even if I were single, you and I would never be together. I'm sorry.

> Sincerely,
> Elizabeth Beckwith

Sam Lipsyte

Dear Sam:
Are the lack of Christmas light fuses a conspiracy to get me to buy
new strings of lights every year? Does it look like I have sucker on
my forehead?

> *Sue Viola*
> *Vancouver, BC*

Dear Sue:
Did you mean "a" sucker on your forehead? I'd need to meet
you or see a photograph before I could really answer this
question. But if you did have a sucker on your forehead,
something moist and squidlike, say, I would probably have
trouble dating you, not that you have that in mind, and
I'm married anyway, but I could not help feeling the erotic

charge of your letter. Or maybe it was all that talk about "fuses."

Sam

. . .

Dear Sam:
Has there ever been a Jewish midget?

Jaime L.
Marion, OH

Dear Jaime:

Are you thinking of Eddie Carmel, the Jewish giant, made famous by a photograph taken by Diane Arbus? Probably not, I'm guessing, or you would have asked about Jewish giants. I've begun researching this question and found a rich vein of material from startlingly moronic people on the Internet. Apparently, the really dumb racists and anti-Semites and midget-haters like to talk about "Jewish midgets" from many (and mostly demeaning) perspectives. But I'm assuming you are not part of that sordid world and simply want an honest answer to an honest question. So, offhand, I know of only a few Jewish midgets: Bill Gates, Jeff Goldblum, Elle Fanning, and Barack Obama.

Sam

. . .

Dear Sam:

My boyfriend's name is Dan, which is inconveniently right next to "Dad" in my cell phone contact list. My tipsy fingers acciden-tally sent a racy text message to my father instead of my boyfriend yesterday. What should I do? Act like it never happened?

> *Tipsy*
> *Tallahassee, FL*

Dear Tipsy:

I think you should act like it did happen, but only under the condition that you can set up some hidden cameras and let your boyfriend in on it and then really press the issue, pre-tend the "sext" wasn't an accident, and figure out an uproari-ous way to "punk" or "Punk'd" your father, exposing him in all his awkward, incest-minded loneliness, and then use that clip in Hollywood as a "calling card." Finally, when it's all over, you can get some therapy and find out why you need to date men whose names are so close to the word "Dad."

> Sam

...

Dear Sam:

I loved Quangaroos the cereal, but it's off the market. Is there a way that maybe I could get the recipe and start manufacturing it for those of us who still crave Quangaroos?

> *Ray Allen*
> *Hobbs, NM*

Dear Ray:

It's a brilliant idea. I'm assuming you have a lot of experience with industrial espionage and large-scale breakfast cereal manufacture and this excites me. I think you've located the niche that's been right under our goddamn noses all along. Quangaroos! Who'd a thunk it? Fucking Ray Allen out of Hobbs, New Mexico did. Sonofabitch. I'm good for half the start-up money. Let's get crackin'! This could inspire the nation. Nobody will remember Ray Allen the basketball star ever again.

Sam

. . .

Dear Sam:

I'm working on an online dating site profile. How honest should I be about myself? For example, under "hobbies," I've listed "scrapbooking" and "country line dancing." These are both true, but will it hurt my chances?

Rose

Hutchinson, KS

Dear Rose:

Hurt your chances with whom? With scrapbooking, country-line-dancing George Clooney? With your grandmother? If you want to find somebody to share these activities with (and, to be honest, I'm not sure what either of them is) then you should leave it in your profile. If you still want a chance at life you should delete them at once.

Sam

. . .

Dear Sam:
What will I be? Will I be pretty? Will I be rich? (I'm fifteen.)
Margaret
Queens, NY

Dear Margaret:
You're fifteen so you already know whether you'll be pretty. You never had a choice in the matter. But whether you'll be rich is entirely up to you. Don't let those naysayers and doom-and-gloomers get you down with their gobbledy-gook about the stagnant wages of the last decade, or the myth of class fluidity, or the concentration of most of the nation's wealth at the very top. If you really, really, really, really want to be rich, you can be. Of course, it would help if you were pretty. This is true of men and women both, by the way.

Sam

Paul Simms

Dear Paul:

My Japanese business colleagues have invited me out for an evening of karaoke. Is there any special etiquette I should follow?

Katy Sanner
Spanish Fork, UT

Dear Katy:

In Japan, the most important aspect of karaoke is not performance, but rather audience participation—preferably in a call-and-response style. Which is why the most popular karaoke song in Japan is Cam'ron's 2000 hit "What Means the World to You?" Over a sample of "Roxanne" by The Police, you will call out, "What means the world to you?" and your business colleagues will reply, "My money, my dough, my hos, my clothes." You requery: "What means the world to you?" The reply? "Lots of cheese, shopping sprees." Now is not the time to lay back in the cut, so ask again, "What means the world to you?" By now, people are up on the tables screaming, "Some sex, some mex, and a little bit of ex."

(I'm assuming your business colleagues are from Tokyo. If they're from Osaka—or the more southern region—just stick with that Tubes song "What Do You Want from Life?" This is the second most revered karaoke song in Japan. The Japanese will even be able to keep up with you during that long list at the end, which includes—among other things—a kidney-shaped swimming pool, a personally autographed picture of Randy Mantooth, and a baby's arm holding an apple.)

Paul

. . .

Dear Paul:
I consider myself to be a fairly private person. I don't like sharing my triumphs or concerns with anyone—even with my closest friends. Recently, though, I had to undergo a hysterectomy and I feel the need to discuss the issue with the people who've been there and supported me the longest. Would it be okay to do so via Facebook or Twitter? I'm tired and would rather take care of this all at once. This is all new to me.

Melia Patz
Lufkin, TX

Dear Melia:

You have one friend who consistently seems to take the news of your health difficulties even harder than you do. She calls often to "check in" on you, and right after she hangs up she calls all your other friends, updates them, and then says, "I can't talk right now—I'm too upset about what's going on with Melia." In a few years, you and all your friends will realize what a load she is and you'll all decide to freeze her out. But for now, letting her disseminate information about your progress is a more effective and dignified way of updating everyone than Twittering about it would be.

Paul

. . .

Dear Paul:

I hit a dog with my car yesterday. It didn't die immediately and was able to hobble down the street, but I think it probably died later. Should I tell my girlfriend?

Frank
Detroit, MI

Dear Frank:

No need to tell your girlfriend. I told her already. She was troubled by your behavior—and more than a little hurt that you would keep this from her. I told her that you just might not be at a place in your life where you're able to make a commitment to honesty just yet. It's probably best if you give her a little space right now. She and I are going out for coffee later this week to try to talk this all out, in a purely platonic way, and also I want to introduce her to the puppy I just adopted from the special-needs pound.

Paul

. . .

Dear Paul:

I've been going to the steakhouse on the corner for damn near twelve years and they've always gotten everything just right. Medium, just how I like it. But this week, three nights in a row, they got the medium thing wrong. Blood was running everywhere. What's a polite way to ask for a better steak?

Jackson P.

Daytona Beach, FL

Dear Jackson:

It's been taken care of. Jackson? Jackson? I took care of it, okay? I went over there yesterday and had a little talk with these fuckers. Turns out there was a . . . let's say . . . a "language barrier" with the Mexican guy who works the broiler. Also, his papers weren't in order. So he's gone now, and his little buddies know they're on thin ice too if this happens again. Enjoy your steak.

Paul

. . .

Dear Paul:
Mad Men is my favorite show. Where can I get a cool suit like Don Draper?

Jeff P.

Dear Jeff:
The season three *Mad Men* boxed set actually comes with a Don Draper suit, which has been shrink-wrapped down to the size of a small wallet. These are the same shrink-wrapped Don Draper suits they shoot into the audience from a T-shirt cannon during commercial breaks during the Golden Globes. One year, Guy Pearce got nailed right in the nuts by one of these, but he ended up being a pretty good sport about it.

Paul

...

Dear Paul:
I hate Mad Men. Am I missing something? Why all the excitement?

Marsha
Meyers Lake, OH

Dear Marsha:
Here's what you're missing: The title *Mad Men* is both a pun on the fact that the main characters are "ad men"

(men who work in advertising) and a reference to Madison Avenue (where many advertising firms had their offices in the 1960s). The "Mad" part also has two other meanings: "mad" as in angry, and "mad" as in insane, or suffering from madness. If you keep these four hidden meanings in mind, you will be able to enjoy the show.

Also, don't be embarrassed. Many TV shows are a rather brutal slog until the word puzzles of their titles are unlocked. *Bosom Buddies,* for example, is virtually incomprehensible to viewers who haven't "unpacked" that the title refers both to the closeness of the main characters' friendship, and also to the fact that they use fake women's bosoms to hide in the girls-only hotel or whatever the fuck that place was supposed to be. And *Happy Days* is as impenetrable as an art film to viewers who never figure out that it's about the exploits of the Day family in their hometown of Happy, Wisconsin.

Furthermore, I just have to say this: Every five years or so, I try to enjoy a Saul Bellow novel. It never works. *Augie March?* Nothing. *Humboldt's Gift?* Nothing. This has been going on for twenty-five years. I would have given up a long time ago, but when you have Martin Amis and Philip Roth and James Wood (and Woods) going on about how great Saul Bellow is, you can't just shrug the guy off. Last month, feeling certain that by now—middle-aged and steeped in regrets—I would finally have the maturity to appreciate his work, I read *Seize the Day*. Ugh.

The same goes for the Final Fantasy series of video games and Halo multiplayer. Also, truffles and truffle oil. And Vampire Weekend.

So my advice is: If you're twenty-five or younger, loudly proclaim your disdain for this and any other things that everyone else likes but you don't as a badge of honor. If you're over twenty-five, just sit quietly till the conversation shifts to a different topic.

Paul

Laraine Newman

Dear Laraine:
This is incredibly embarrassing, but I don't know who else to ask.
For some reason, my genitals smell like onions. I have excellent
hygiene, and I've tried scrubbing down there repeatedly, to no
avail. Obviously, I don't get a lot of oral sex because there aren't
many ladies who enjoy a male member that stinks of onions. What
should I do?!

Anonymous
Tallahassee, FL

Dear Anonymous:
As you've chosen not to reveal anything about yourself,
I'm going to go out on a limb here and guess that you're
Italian or of some other Mediterranean lineage. It's been

proven that cultural preferences can permeate everything. Everything. Furthermore, I would venture to say that you come from a lower socioeconomic background. Am I right? Scary, huh? You see, your problem isn't that unusual, but because you live in a place like Tallahassee, where the population is predominantly white, Anglo-Saxon, and Baptist, perhaps you've encountered genitals that smelled like buttermilk biscuits, or fatback. This can be an innocuous scent to those who are used to more pungent aromas and would go unnoticed by someone like you. Therefore, you would surmise that yours are the only genitals with any kind of odor.

Now, let me address the socioeconomic part of the equation. Have you ever heard the expression "A leek is a poor man's asparagus"? Indeed there are different levels of aromatic allium that are associated with class. For instance, I come from an upper-middle-class background, so my genitals smell like shallots, so often used in French cuisine. If one were middle class, a scallion might represent their junk odor. Anonymous, you simply come from a long line of onion eaters and that's nothing to be ashamed of. Find yourself a nice Italian or Greek girl. For her, your business will smell like home.

Laraine

. . .

Dear Laraine:

I keep the Velvet Underground on my iPod. I don't listen to it, it's just there in case someone goes snooping around in my music, so that I look cool. What other music should I load in there to seem cool?

Jeff Campbell
Bushkill, PA

Dear Jeff:

You can't please everyone. To try and second-guess the snooper is a nonstarter because it's such a broad spectrum. What if "someone" were, oh, say, your mom, since you're so clearly an adolescent. I know, I know, who cares if your mom thinks you're cool, right? Well, it's just good politics to endear yourself to Ms. Dinner McCreditcard, bro. Now, your mom's criteria might be retro, but not just any retro. It has to be *her* retro. What if, for her, that's The Captain and Tennille? Then you're faced with the possibility that one of your buds is snooping, looking for something he thinks is cool, like maybe Pretty Lights, but then he comes across "Muskrat Love." How are you going to explain that? And what if a miracle happens and a girl is snooping in your room? She's only going to think a band like Kaskade is cool. But if you have him on your iPod and one of your other buds sees that, he's going to think you're gay. To quote Shakespeare, "What a tangled web we weave, when first we practice to deceive."

Jeff, the fact that you're that studied in your attempt to be cool in absentia is just sad. Also, Jeff, here's another Shakespeare quote: "To thine own self be true." Put your own tunes on there, for heaven's sake! It just better not be anything by Train, because that IS gay.

> Your pal,
> Laraine

. . .

Dear Laraine:

I am terrified of buttons. This is, in fact, a common phobia called "koumpounophobia," so I am not a freak. But I would like to be able to undress my boyfriend and wear cute cardigans. What should I do?

> *Janet Bayne*
> *Sonoma, CA*

Dear Janet:

I hate to say this, but there was a time when I felt that obscure phobias were a tactic lonely people devised to call undue attention to themselves. However, it turns out my aunt Lovey had the exact same phobia. Here are some things she tried that may work for you:

1) Gloves (for some, it's a texture thing).

2) Aunt Lovey took a page from Perseus's playbook when approaching Medusa. Direct visual contact with buttons was traumatic for her, so with my help and the help

of our neighbor's son who is in his third year at MIT, we fashioned the "koumpounonator": a padded harness that fit easily on both shoulders with rear- and side-view mirrors attached. I BeDazzled it for a nice fashion touch.

3) In my brilliant career as a performer, I've often enjoyed the luxury of having others dress me. For Aunt Lovey's seventy-eighth birthday, I sprang for her own personal wardrobe assistant when she wanted to have an assignation with her boyfriend. Even though Aunt Lovey couldn't personally undress Irving, Sheila (a very nice "up-and-comer" in the design world) removed Irving's Brooks Brothers shirt to the tune of "bolero." Ring-a-ding-ding! Afterward, I felt I owed Sheila "a little something extra" since she reported to me that Irving's genitals smelled like herring.

Laraine

...

Dear Laraine:
Sometimes I find myself ever so slightly turned on by the juniper tree in my backyard. I am worried about how this might develop. What can you suggest to nip this in the bud (no pun intended)?

Lucille Klasko
Lansing, MI

Dear Lucille:
You're wise to be circumspect when it comes to a juniper. They're notorious players. My friend Andrea was involved

with a redwood (for obvious reasons) that was the strong and silent type. Reliable. Unfortunately for Andrea, reliable meant boring. The redwood was sharing a space with a juniper and she couldn't take her eyes off it. The juniper knew exactly what it was doing, and before long Andrea found herself seduced and abandoned. But not before the juniper had really messed with her head. Andrea had always been sensitive about her weight, and once the juniper had her where it wanted her, Andrea told me how it dropped subtle hints about how fetching the willow sapling next door was. I mean, who can compete with that, right? What a dick.

I have boundless admiration for you. It's hard enough to resist the attraction. But to seek to arrest it, when you've already felt stirrings "down there," is a monumental act of will. The proximity of your juniper makes it especially challenging. Honestly, Lucille, it's an inside job. Just know that you're playing with fire....Fire...Hmmmm.

Laraine

...

Dear Laraine:
If I were a zebra I think I'd be kind of irked at my so-called cam-
ouflage. Don't you think nature could've done a little better?

Lynn K.S.
Ann Arbor, MI

Dear Lynn:

I have to agree. However, there's a buttload of things ahead in the line when it comes to nature's errors. There are animals with excellent camouflage that really don't deserve it. Like human evil. Look at how handsome Richard Ramirez and Ted Bundy were. Also, cats. Cats are so pretty, but we all know how worthless they are.

Laraine

Jerri Blank

Dear Jerri:

I have an unspecial birthday: New Year's Day. Because my birth-
day is so terribly close to this dreadful "official" holiday, I suffer
the terrible setback of receiving dual-purpose gifts. What should I
do, save finding new friends and family?

Fred Dobson
Portland, ME

Dear Fred:
You sound like a real crybaby. You are what we in the
slammer call a pussy. You know what, Fred? Even outside
the slammer you're a pussy. "I suffer the terrible setback of
receiving dual-purpose gifts." Boo hoo. Let me tell you about
terrible setbacks, Fred. I like to gamble. I also enjoy blood-

shed, which is why more often than not you'll find me in the front row of a cockfight. So, this one night after a hilariously brutal match, some words were exchanged between me and a wiley one-legged Mexican named Vasquez. I don't want to go into the amusingly gruesome details, but let's just say I soon found myself with a corpse. Nobody's fault; these things happen. Anywhosil, I was thinkin' I could just drag the carcass over to that abandoned lot across the alley, dig a shallow grave, cover it with some debris, and *hasta mañana.* But get this—before I could get *el muerto Mexicano* out the door, a sleet storm hit, covering the ground with ice and making it harder than a Chinaman's skull. Eventually I had to drag him about twelve blocks so I could dump him in an incinerator. So my advice to you, Fred, is to save those tears for a real problem.

Jerri

...

Dear Jerri:
I have this friend; we will just call her "Dani" for the purpose of this letter. She tends to smell quite awful, and I just can't stand it anymore. How can I ask her to improve her smell without hurting her feelings?

> *Holding Her Nose in*
> *California,*
> *Camille L.*

Dear Camille:

Do you own a hose? Most of the best delousings I've ever received were when I was gettin' hosed down in the joint. You'd be surprised at the places that water can reach, especially if it's coming at you with the brutal force of a typhoon. Sometimes I'd get in line for seconds. So I suggest that you hose her down. Or better yet, plant some screamers on her and then drop a dime. Let the state take care of your stinky problem for you. By the time your friend hits the street, the state will have graciously eliminated your stinky problem. Of course, the downside is she will have permanent physical and emotional scarring. That *is* a downside, right?

Jerri

. . .

Dear Jerri:

I really want a pet. What do you think would be best? I live in the city, and someone recommended one of those small poodles to me. They're supposed to be really portable and hypoallergenic. What if I named the poodle something kind of tough, like Frank or Kevin? Alternately, a betta fish could be nice. Or maybe a turtle?

Becky Perlman
Chicago, IL

Dear Becky:

As you might know, I like snakes. I'm also partial to burros. I did a donkey show in Tijuana. But here's the thing: pets weigh you down. They're like those kids who ride the special bus. They never really grow up and they always depend on you. Do you really want that kind of aggravation? If I were you, I'd get me one of those babies from the black market. Not only will they keep you company, but you know what else you got, Becky? You got an *investment*. Do you have any idea what young adults bring on the black market, Beck? I'm not sayin' you have to sell it back, but isn't it nice to know that's an option? Even if you're sure you don't want to unload the kid, you could still pretend you might. I think you'll be pleasantly surprised by just how far a little black-market threat talk goes in keeping a kid in line.

Jerri

. . .

Dear Jerri:

I'm a nineteen-year-old college sophomore at the University of Wisconsin–Madison. As a native New Yorker, I'm finding the transition between a population obsessed with salads and ephedrine to one that hungers for cheese curds and mayonnaise a bit troubling on my waistline. I was wondering if you had any low-calorie recipes that you could prescribe for college students like myself.

Eating like a Fatty
McFatster

Dear Fatty:

Listen, tubbo, when I lived in the box at the Florida pen for shivving a Cuban in the shower, I lived on nothing but corn bread and water. Corn bread in the morning, corn bread in the afternoon, and corn bread again at night. Here's a recipe for you, blubber: have some of your bunkies lock your fat ass in a metal box and then stick it out in the hot sun. They'll think of it as a prank, you can sweat out some of that bloat, and I could stop receiving ridiculous letters like this from you. Everybody wins.

Jerri

Paul Scheer

Dear Paul:

My boyfriend wants to get another tattoo on his arm, completing what he's calling a "full sleeve." I'm a little worried about this. I've seen those old navy guys with tattoos so blue they look like bruises. In another thirty years, is my boyfriend just going to look like he has leprosy?

Angie P.
Chicago, IL

Dear Angie:
If your boyfriend wants to get a full sleeve, I suggest he get a tattoo of an actual shirtsleeve. That way, he'll be fulfilling *his* need for ink and *your* need to be with someone presentable in public. For example, not only do I have shirtsleeves tattooed on both of my arms, but I also have cargo pants

tattooed on my legs and thighs so I'm never not dressed. As far as looking like a bruised navy guy, every dude will look like that someday. That's just a fact.

Paul

...

Dear Paul:
I just adopted a pair of adorable pugs and I'm thinking about naming them after two characters from The Magic Flute, *Papageno and Papagena. My wife claims this is pretentious and that nobody will get the reference. Who's right?*

Opera Lover
New York, NY

Dear Opera Lover:
I have bad news for you. Your wife is a robot sent from the future to kill you. Her fatal flaw is not "getting" pretentious pop-culture references. Eliminate her immediately! Save yourself and humanity!

Paul

...

Dear Paul:
Lately, my wife has been repeatedly asking me, "Does this outfit make me look fat?" I really don't know how to answer her. Didn't Freud

*say that self-perception is an illusion of the ego? How can I honestly
say if she does or doesn't "look" fat without acknowledging that my
perception of the outside world might just be a fantasy of my own
brain? I mean, would she ask George Berkeley if she looked fat?*

> *Darren R.*
> *Santa Fe, NM*

Dear Darren:
Let's face it, you are a chubby chaser. We all know it and it's
totally cool. No need to hide behind big words and obscure
references. Embrace your fetish.

> Paul

...

Dear Paul:
*Is there such a thing as love at first sight, or is he just looking at
my tits?*

> *Nicole*
> *Petaluma, CA*

Dear Nicole:
Ugh! How many times do I have to explain this to you? I
wasn't looking at your tits, I was looking at your really cool
retro T-shirt. Your "tits" just got in the way, but also made
that image of Fat Albert look 3-D. Hence the staring.

> Paul

...

Dear Paul:
I want to quit my horrible, soul-sucking job and finally finish
writing my novel, but my friends keep telling me it's a terrible idea
because of the recession. Are they just afraid I might be successful
and they'll have to accept that they're probably trapped forever in
their unfulfilling, non-novel-writing jobs?

> *A Frustrated Writer*
> *Austin, TX*

Dear Frustrated Writer:
When it comes to writing, I'll say this much. If it's not
written by Mike "The Situation" Sorrentino or Sarah Palin,
I'm not reading it. And I think most of the country agrees
with me. DOWN WITH BOOKS!!! BURN! BURN!
BURN!

> Paul

...

Dear Paul:
Is it okay to break up with someone on Twitter? What if I don't
have a Twitter account and I ask a friend to do it for me? What's
the protocol?

> *Stacie*
> *Orlando, FL*

Dear Stacie:

As my good friend Kathleen Turner once told me, "GET OUT OF MY HOUSE, YOU FREAKY STALKER!" But that's beside the point. Yes, it is okay to break up over Twitter. If you don't have a Twitter account, here is one other option for breaking up: send a mass text to everyone but the dude (or gal) you're dating. Skywriting always works. It's public and so much fun. But I think the absolute best way is a singing telegram. It's just not possible to be upset when a man in a gorilla costume tells you, "Stacie don't love you no more," to the tune of "Eleanor Rigby."

Paul

...

Dear Paul:

I'm curious about sushi, but the whole raw aspect of it kinda freaks me out. What's the difference between eating raw fish and just a big plate of parasites and bacteria?

Fearful Eater
San Diego, CA

Dear Fearful Eater:

The difference is you use soy sauce on one and the other you eat plain. Enjoy!

Paul

Rob Baedeker

Dear Rob:
What advice can you offer me in the event that I find myself trapped for several hours with my mortal enemy inside, say, a meat locker or a bank vault?

Paul Raabe

Dear Paul:
Stay calm, and then shoot him/her in the heart with a crossbow. Good luck!

Rob

. . .

Dear Rob:

Who's the funkiest of the bunch? James Brown, Rick James, or Jeff "Skunk" Baxter, the guitarist from the Doobie Brothers?

> *Gary Gruppo*
> *Atwood, KS*

Dear Gary:

Hi, Jeff! It's you, right, Skunk? Love the pseudonym! (Gruppo, as in "Gruppo guys rockin' out and 'smokin' grass"? Very trippy, Jeff. Nice.) Clever move to include yourself on that list and thereby imply you're in the same category as the Jameses, but you kind of shoot yourself in the foot with the part that explains who you are (really lowers your status compared with the other two). Anyway, good luck with the missile defense consulting career (I Wikipedia'd you!).

> Rob

...

Dear Rob:

In ten words or less, could you please explain how the current Israel/Palestinian situation can finally be resolved once and for all? Just something simple, so we can all get on with our lives? Thanks much.

> *Rebecca Owen*
> *Ann Arbor, MI*

Dear Rebecca:
Give both sides penguins. Everyone loves penguins.

Rob

. . .

Dear Rob:
In your opinion, what are the lamest Guinness World Records to hold? Conversely, what are the best records?

Simon B.

Dear Simon:
Lamest Records:

—Longest penis, held by my ex's current lover, what's-his-name.

—Richest magician/inventor, held by same guy. Oh, I believe he's called René. Kind of a lame name for a dude, right?

Best Records:

—Most holes punched in drywall during a dinner party (not an official category, yet, but I am petitioning Guinness).

Rob

. . .

Dear Rob:

I recently visited the South of France. I highly recommend it. I don't have a question, I just thought you might want a suggestion for a travel destination. If you need more suggestions, just let me know.

Celia Jarden
Star Valley, NE

Dear Celia:

Really? The South of France? Aren't you worried that by mentioning it here it'll get discovered? Is it even accessible by normal transportation, or do you have to hire a "native guide" to get there? *Muchas gracias,* asshole!

Rob

. . .

Dear Rob:

I'm on the threshold of what may be my best work, but I've begun to struggle with the dreaded writer's block. The beginning just fell onto the page, but now my ideas are starting to dry up and I feel like I'm straying from my original premise. So tell me, how would you write the autobiography of my life?

Judith Foxley
Waco, TX

Dear Judith:

How would I write the autobiography of your life. WTF, Judith?! I guess I would transmigrate my soul into your body when you were a baby and then just make all the same life decisions you did, except at the very end I'd enroll in a memoir-writing course at the Learning Annex.

Rob

. . .

Dear Rob:

I love the movie Mary Poppins *but can't stand Dick Van Dyke's horrible fake Cockney accent. How can I watch the movie without this bothering me?*

Amanda

Sun City, AZ

Dear Amanda:

No offense, but this topic bores the tits off me. I literally have fallen asleep twice trying to make it to the end of your question. Here's what you do: two tablespoons each of rosemary, lemon zest, and salt. Rub olive oil all over a whole chicken, sprinkle the lemon mixture on, and then bake at 375 for about an hour. It's delicious. That's got nothing to do with *Mary Poppins*—I'm just trying to offer somethin' useful to save face for us both. Blimey!

Rob

. . .

Dear Rob:

I have this theory that you should never trust a man who points with his pinkie. Agreed? Who else should I not trust?

Mike

New Orleans, LA

Dear Mike:

The Buddha said, "He who seeks out others not to trust is a dickshine par excellence."

Mike, you seem to have a lot going for you—you developed your own "theory" and you got it together to send in this question. Now bend your own pinkie backward and look who it's pointing at. Try to show yourself some compassion, and then you may feel less of a need to nitpick the faults of others.

Rob

P.S. Technically it should be "Whom else should I not trust?" Peace.

Dan Guterman

Dear Dan:

What is the protocol when an acquaintance Tweets or posts on Facebook a notification that a relative or friend has died? I generally ignore, because I disagree in principle with a 140-character obituary. And yet I find that a lot of people respond with condolences and hearts made out of a greater-than sign and a "3."

Alana

Brooklyn, NY

Dear Alana:

Tweeting about the passing of a loved one, or breaking the news via Facebook, is, as far as I'm concerned, wholly inappropriate. After all, that's what unsolicited mass e-mails are for. But to answer your question, here is the protocol I most often proceed with when responding to an online death notice. First, communicate your grief with an appropriately mournful emoticon. Use as many ampersands, semicolons, and open parentheses as are needed to fully convey your anguish. Next, when it comes to expressing your condolences, you can never go wrong with a tasteful arrangement of virtual flowers. Retreat to your FarmVille plot and harvest a respectful bouquet of daffodils to send by way of Facebook. Or—if you've managed to unlock Level 35— some sober white lilies. Lastly, the best way to console a grieving e-friend is to share your own personal story of loss. For instance, the time your Sims-wife passed away and how you thought you'd never be whole again. Until, three days later, when you designed a brand-new Sims-wife.

Dan

. . .

Dear Dan:
All these years later and I still don't get it: What's the difference between a stalagmite and a stalactite?

Lorna Hertzog
Muncie, IN

Dear Lorna:
Thank you for taking the time during what I assume is another weekend spent spelunking to write in with your

dilemma. Stalactites are conical deposits that form at the roof of a cave and hang downward, while stalagmites are deposits that form on the bottom of a cave and grow upward. However, there are other, more important differences as well. Stalactites, when alluded to in a humorous grotto-related anecdote, will often solicit an amused, openmouthed response from cocktail party guests. On the other hand, droll musings about stalagmites will likely produce a muted smile at best. Additionally, while both terms may appear quite similar at first blush, each has its own unique way of being spelled.

Dan

...

Dear Dan:
Is there a manly way in which to eat cotton candy? If so, I'd like to find out what it is.
Thanks.

Keenan R.
Baltimore, MD

Dear Keenan:
The masculine consumption of outwardly whimsical foodstuffs can pose a definite challenge. Cotton candy in particular, with its dazzling pink color and fanciful appearance, presents a number of obstacles. Here is what I suggest:

Walk up to the nearest cotton candy vendor and order your-self a single serving of the gently spun sugar snack. Now, as you wait for the emasculating treat to be prepared, change into a rustic flannel shirt of large-print lumberjack plaid. If at all possible, grow a thick beard as you wait. Also, if there are any imposing trees nearby, go ahead and chop those down as well. These first initial steps, though simple in execution, are critical in offsetting the castrating effects of consuming cotton candy.

Once suited in virile plaid, and having impressed onlookers with your dominion over nature, it is time to transport the carnival snack into your mouth in the least feminine way possible. Start with a single bite of the cotton candy. Without missing a beat, let your face fall in horrifying disappointment. Remark aloud how you're "pretty sure" you asked that the cotton candy be prepared "medium-rare." Do not worry if this makes no sense what-soever, as it will still sound like a manly thing to say. The next four to five bites should be taken in rapid succession, preferably while reshingling a roof, firing a rifle wildly into the air, or performing a feat of jaw-dropping athleticism, such as pole-vaulting. Once those activities are complete, finish off the sugary-sweet cone and dispel any remaining skepticism concerning your manhood by carrying out the most courageous act imaginable: riding the nearby Ferris wheel.

Dan

...

Dear Dan:

For ecological purposes, I wear my clothes for three days. Then I flip them inside out and wear them for three more days. Yet, still, I feel as if I'm not getting the full amount of wear out of my clothes. How could I possibly extend this cycle?

> *J.L.*
> *Dallas, TX*

Dear J.L.:

Before we begin, let me first applaud your conservation efforts as far as your nom de plume is concerned. It brings me great joy to see such a selfless act, especially when so many other Americans are needlessly burning through our nation's vowel-and-consonant supply. (Yes, I'm looking at you, Brittnee.) As far as your clothes-based predicament is concerned, have you tried doing away with your outer-wear altogether? If not, give it a shot! Also, give sending me where it is you live and routinely walk around during the day a try. Which reminds me, are you of the female persuasion?

> Dan

...

Dear Dan:

My girlfriend accuses me of having "no class" because every once in a while I enjoy snacking while seated on the toilet. Can't a guy just relax and eat some potato chips while multitasking?

Joel Holden
Erie, PA

To Whom It May Concern:
Please unsubscribe me from this Sedaratives mailing list. Thank you.

Dan

Anthony Jeselnik

Dear Anthony:
How do you get those little pills off of your sweaters? It's driving
me crazy.

> *Leanne Brown*
> *Lamplighter, NH*

Dear Leanne:

First you have to get rid of any pets you might have. Cats, dogs, birds, even fish. They've all got to go. All done? Great, now I can answer your question. To get those little pills off of your sweaters, just pick the pills off one by one with your fingernails whenever you find yourself trapped in a boring conversation. Worst-case scenario: conversation over. Best-case scenario: your boring friend will start helping you with their own fingers! As for the back of your sweater, well, I'm afraid you're just going to have to throw the back of that sweater away.

Anthony

...

Dear Anthony:
Let's get this straight: I like drinking. I like it a lot. But don't you think just liking it shouldn't necessarily label you an alcoholic? What's a bottle or two of wine while watching The Biggest Loser*? It's nothing, right?*

Sarge Collins
Newport Beach, CA

Dear Sarge:
You are correct. Drinking a bottle of wine or two while watching *The Biggest Loser* is NOTHING. You should really step it up to at least two entire boxes of wine per episode. I recommend going with a nice Franzia white zinfandel during the show and then below-average Franzia Chianti during commercials as an emotional cleanser. Also, you should be able to rest easy knowing that alcoholics don't actually "like" drinking, they just really hate watching the morbidly obese make a mockery of the elliptical machine.

Anthony

...

Dear Anthony:
I find the fig confusing. Why does it only have one cookie named after it? It's freaking delicious.

> *Gary Saperstein*
> *Manhasset, NY*

Dear Gary:
I take it you wrote this letter after eating one fig, but before eating a second fig. Everyone loves the first fig they eat, not understanding that they've hit their fig threshold. Then they'll usually try to eat a second fig, thinking that they've discovered a miracle fruit and cursing their parents for keeping the fig from them as children. But, trust me, once that second fig hits your lips, you'll realize the truth. Figs are disgusting. They are like giant raisins filled with sugar and they are the consistency of a mummified ball sack. That is why the only people who actually do eat figs are the elderly, because they're atoning for their numerous sins and preparing themselves for hell. Hell, by the way, is an endless fig-eating contest.

> Anthony

...

Dear Anthony:
I recently lost 115 pounds. Where is my Subway endorsement? All I got rid of is my type 2 diabetes. So what? Can you help me exploit my fine health?

> *Gina Boccadora*
> *Bonnano, NJ*

Dear Gina:

I don't know where your Subway endorsement is. I called their corporate offices and they've never even heard of you. I even told them about your funny "type 2 diabetes" joke, but the guy on the phone actually suffers from type 2 diabetes, so he got mad and put me on with his supervisor, or "supervisor artist" as they like to be called. I once again explained your situation, and he didn't even believe that you lost 115 pounds. And now neither do I. He was very convincing.

Anthony

. . .

Dear Anthony:

As I watched the news last night, buried deep into the second half, just before sports, they talked about a dude who had his AIDS cured. Shouldn't that be bigger news than the guy at 7-Eleven who ate six of those sausage dogs in a row and then ran out without paying?

Michael Miglianico
Arles, TX

Dear Michael:

Are you serious? Six sausage dogs in a row? And then he just took off? That's unbelievable from both security and dietary standpoints. 7-Eleven clerks keep those sausages on rollers behind two-foot-high quarter-inch Plexiglas, so unless he's Stretch Armstrong, he's not getting six sausage dogs without help from the clerk. And no 7-Eleven clerk worth his Basic brand menthol cigarettes is just going to hand a customer one sausage dog, much less six sausage dogs, without asking for payment before watching them disappear down some miracle throat.

So, yeah, considering AIDS has been cured since Magic Johnson led the Dream Team to a gold medal in the '92 Olympics, I'd say Stretch Armstrong robbing a 7-Eleven is the bigger story.

Anthony

Scott Thompson

Dear Scott:
The grass is always greener on the other side, right? Then basically
no one is happy?

Bob M.
Morton, TX

Dear BM:

I call you "BM" because I'm turning your name into an amusing acronym, much like the esteemed sex advice columnist Dan Savage would do. I chose these two letters because in my part of the world "BM" means "bowel movement." Amusing, no? I'm going to say Dan Savage's name again so that it is more likely to turn up in his Google Alert, making him mention it in his "Dan Savage" column, thus doubling the potential publicity for my new graphic novel, *Danny Husk: Hollow Planet.* Does that answer your question?

Scott

...

Dear Scott:

If Devo are not men but Devo, then what exactly are men? Or Devo for that matter?

Confused Student
New York, NY

Dear Confused Student:

I remember when I was a young confused student and I went to a Devo concert on one of their first tours. I don't remember anything except pogoing to the very lyrics you are evoking and realizing that I understood what they were singing about. Unfortunately I was too high and don't remember what it was.

Scott

...

Dear Scott:

I just killed a moth in my home. But now I feel guilty, because I've heard that moths are a dead person coming to visit me. Is it okay that I killed it? Also, if it's a relative or loved one, should it be a butterfly?

Angela N.
Sydney, Australia

Dear Angela N.:

First of all, it's okay to kill a moth because it's an insect and it's okay to kill all insects and most reptiles. You can still kill fish with impunity but that's going to end soon. It's pretty much impossible to kill a mammal of any kind nowadays for sport, even mice. You can't make a simple crush video anymore and expect to get away with it. It's coming to the point where you won't even be able to kill a vicious predator in self-defense. Everybody will be all, "Couldn't you just have talked to the bear?" Second, yes, it is true that a moth is a dead person coming to visit you. What we don't understand yet is what happens to moths when they die. Do they come back as people? And if they do, then is murder okay? Third, loved ones can be butterflies but they have to be related to you by blood. The one you killed is probably just a dead friend of some sort. The good thing is that if he or she does come back as a person, then you have the chance to make it up to them for killing them when they were moths.

Scott

...

Dear Scott:

I am on the "new money" side of a prominent Boston street and I have some blue-blood "old money" friends of the family coming over for aperitifs and a light luncheon. My problem is that since the renovation of my brownstone, the old servants' entrance was sealed

and I simply cannot have the caterers enter through the front door
in front of the blue bloods. What to do?

David

Dear David:

You're going to have to disguise all the caterers as blue
bloods. First of all, put them on a diet of champagne, her-
oin, and toast points so they get the proper pallor. Then
dress them all in very fancy clothes. Don't be afraid of top
hats. And, finally, disguise all the food, cutlery, etc., as tiny
dogs. When the cater waiters pull off their disguises at the
appropriate time, the silly toffs will just think that they
teleported in out of nowhere and will chow down none
the wiser.

Scott

. . .

Dear Scott:
I need a little dental work done. Any suggestions?

Todd Day
Homosassa, FL

Dear Todd:

Why not just save the money and ruin your face so that it
matches your horrible teeth? It's easy, too. Just drag your
face over gravel or mark it up with a knife. Burning is also
good, as is acid, although that costs a little more. If you are

afraid of pain, just get addicted to crystal meth and you can tweak your way to hideousness in a matter of weeks. The best part is your teeth will just fall right out, eliminating any need for further work.

Scott

...

Dear Scott:
What's the perfect formula for deskunking a dumb-ass jerk of a cat who got out?

Rob H.
Geneva, WI

Dear Rob H.:
Fill a bathtub with tomato juice. Throw in the smelly cat. Drown the "dumb-ass" and then buy a dog.

Scott

Rose McGowan

Dear Rose:

What's the best wine to serve at a dinner party that says, "If you guys want to turn this into a key party, I wouldn't be opposed"?

Josh
Manchester, NH

Dearest Josh:
A nice bottle of Manischewitz mixed with Rohypnol usually does the trick.

Rose

. . .

Dear Rose:

I've been married for fifteen years, and my wife just announced that she thinks we should get separate beds. Is she trying to tell me something?

> *Peter D.*
> *Baltimore, MD*

Dear Peter:

Yes. Watch out. It starts with separate beds and then the next thing you know you're being fed poison with dinner. I'm thinking she'll use arsenic. It takes a little while to die and it's quite painful. The good news is that once you're autopsied, a bitter almond smell will be released from your body. Once the medical examiner smells that, your death will be ruled a homicide. I know these things; I've seen *CSI,* both the original show and that stupid Miami spin-off. I can't stand *CSI: Miami.* That redheaded dude thinks he's all slick with his dopey sunglasses. Redheaded dudes are not cool.

> Rose

. . .

Dear Rose:

My girlfriend wants a big, fancy wedding, but I'd rather just go to the courthouse and get it over with. Is there a way to compromise, maybe split the difference? Or is that retarded?

> *Reluctant Groom*
> *Chicago, IL*

Dear Reluctant:

When I'm flummoxed, a good night of square dancing really shakes the dumb right out of me. Also, your girlfriend is a total whore.

Rose

. . .

Dear Rose:

I was laid off a few months ago, and my severance check is bigger than I thought—enough to pay my rent and keep me in weed. Remind me why I should be looking for a new job?

B. Henderson

Grand Rapids, MI

Dear B.:

Because eventually the severance pay will run out and you'll have watched everything on TV and you won't be able to afford cable or Netflix anymore and it will be the end of time so no new movies or TV shows will be produced, the weed will run out, and then you will die. So: Stay at it, B. Henderson! You go, America!

Rose

. . .

Dear Rose:

I know office romances are a terrible idea, but I think I'm falling in love with a woman in the next cubicle. Should I let her know how I feel, or keep my emotions a secret?

Lovelorn in Los Angeles

Dear Lovelorn:

Here's how to make her love you: Start out with late-night calls to her house. Don't talk, just breathe. Heavily. Do that about twenty to thirty times a night. After that, make sure you key her car. Scratch "i love you" all over her new Audi. Follow her to the bathroom and slide love notes under the stall. Get a blow-up doll that looks just like her and keep it in your cubicle. If you kiss the doll super hard at least three times a day, she'll become jealous and will see that there is no such thing as life without you.

Rose

. . .

Dear Rose:

My ten-year high school reunion is coming up, and I can't decide if I should attend. I'm one of those people who got bald and fat, and I don't want to make my former friends and classmates feel superior by comparison. Then again, what if they got balder and fatter than me? Is that a gamble worth taking?

In a Quandary in Quebec

Dear Quebec:

Kenny Rogers was a gambler. He gambled like there was no tomorrow. Then he bought a fried-chicken chain. After that, Kenny got too much plastic surgery and couldn't shut his eyes. Sometimes I see him selling the greatest hits of country on those annoying Time-Life commercials. I'm not gonna lie, I have purchased those three hundred–plus country songs. I like to listen to "Lady" while eating Kenny's fine fried chicken. Would you like to know why I am superior to you, Mr. Quebec? Besides the fact that I'll never be bald or fat, I'll also never be Canadian. Thank god for that. Everyone knows Canadians are bald, fat, and superior to no one.

Rose

Bob Saget

Dear Bob:
I decided to enlist in the navy, but I'm a little annoyed with how my dad keeps referring to it as "the family business." How can I serve my country and yet not follow in the footsteps of my asshole career-military father?

> *P. Campball*
> *Amarillo, TX*

Dear P.:
May I call you "P."? You can call me "B." It's hard to live up to your a-hole father's expectations sometimes. He doesn't read this column, does he? There are many ways to serve your country. I know a girl who served her country. She slept with thousands of servicemen. I can hear rim shots as

I type this. You've got to follow your gut. If you have a large stomach, you can definitely follow your gut 'cause it sticks out ahead of the rest of you when you enter a room. I swear, I'm hearing rim shots as I type this. Maybe your dad's not an a-hole. Maybe he loves you and his country very much. I say that sincerely, in case he's going to read this. And he has firearms. Be safe in the navy and when you come home your dad will probably be crazy proud of you. Don't let guys touch you on the poop deck. God in heaven, make these rim shots stop!!!

Bob

...

Dear Bob:
I'm pretty sure my husband is cheating on me. Do I confront him about it, or just have my own extramarital fun? Two can play at this game, right?

Ready for Some Adultery
Huntington Beach, CA

Dear "Ready":
May I call you "Ready"? I'm just kidding. I'd need to see a jpeg of you first. Yeah, it's tough. A lot of people cheat, probably more men than women. I don't think you should do to him what was done to you. I'd try to figure out if you love him enough to work on it and get as honest as you guys can with each other—counseling, nonangry open

talks—and see if you need to leave him. Relationships are tough. If there are kids involved, it gets trickier.

What I meant to say was...bang his brother and his best friend and his boss, and show the tape at his next business meeting. Then start a website with the footage. It'll be the "second chapter" you've been dreaming of. Then stow away on a navy ship and please give the guy in the last letter some decent sex. He's got some real daddy issues.

Bob

...

Dear Bob:

Is Michael Jackson really dead? I mean, he was once married to Lisa Marie Presley, right? And her dad, Elvis, faked his "heart attack" and is currently living in Kalamazoo, Michigan. So it's not illogical to assume that Jacko is just having us on. What do you think?

M. Cox
Cincinnati, OH

Dear M. Cox:
I'm answering this? God forgive me. I just had a colonoscopy, and they gave me propofol to put me under. The last thing I said to the anesthesiologist before I went out was, "This is it." But to answer your question, which was obviously yet another gallows humor attempt about Michael Jackson...No, it wasn't an Andy Kaufman bit. Andy is

sadly gone, and Michael is sadly gone, and it's, well . . . sad. However, after I got the dose of propofol, I have scheduled myself for five more colonoscopies this month. Propofol and a colonoscopy, it's a win-win.

Bob

. . .

Dear Bob:
I really want to be a good Catholic, but sometimes the whole reli-gion thing feels like believing in Santa. It's a comforting myth, but still just a myth. Can you help me believe again?

Borderline Agnostic
Chicago, IL

Dear Borderline:
I can help you believe again. Sit on my lap and tell me what you want for Christmas. Your gift is in my red sack. Wait, are you a man or a woman? Oh, screw it, it's late when I'm writing this. So to maybe answer your question . . . I believe in the "Power of the Myth," as per Joseph Campbell, and I also believe that life is fairly short. So if the myth is comforting, for me it's fine. And over the holidays, women of all denomina-tions told me what they wished for while they were sitting on my lap. You noticing a unifying theme to these answers yet?

Bob

. . .

Dear Bob:

*What's the difference between jujitsu and tae kwon do? And are
you absolutely positive they're not just made-up words?*

> *Tentative Karate Enthusiast*
> *Kansas City, MO*

Dear Tentative:

You are dead-on correct. They are completely made-up words
and do not exist. And the people who practice these supposed
sports, who can no doubt kick my ass, are not real either. Thank
you for asking such an interesting and intelligent question.

> Bob

...

Dear Bob:

Pirates v. the Hamburglar. Who would win?

> *Gabrielle*
> *Memphis, TN*

Dear Gabrielle:

The Hamburglar. He is a sneaky son of a bitch. He ruined
so many great picnics and playdates for Ronald McDonald.
I fear for the safety of pirates everywhere, knowing that that
bastard is still on the loose.

We must find Bin Laden. Or have we? And more importantly, the Hamburglar.

> Bob

. . .

Dear Bob:

A guy I've been dating for the past month told me he wants to be "friends with benefits." What does this mean? What should I tell him?

> Too Friendly for
> My Own Good
> Phoenix, AZ

Dear Too:

Tell him that's cool with you. By "benefits," he means he'd most likely want to make monthly deposits into your bank account. By "friends," it means you'll accept those checks. But no matter what you do, do not ever have sex with him again. Unless you are in the same place as he is. In which case, just watch reruns of *Oprah* tomorrow. Odds are, she'll answer all your questions.

> Bob

. . .

Dear Bob:

My son is getting harassed by bullies at school and I'm not sure how to help him. I'm looking for advice that's somewhere between "Turn the other cheek" and "Kick 'em hard in the balls."

> *Thanks in advance.*
> *Robyn*
> *Charleston, SC*

Dear Robyn:

I have actually been through this. I went to school in Norfolk, Virginia, and in sixth grade a kid harassed me with anti-Semitic comments all year. Being self-loathing, I welcomed them for a while, but eventually couldn't take it anymore. We scheduled a "fight" in the schoolyard after school. He kicked me in the balls and my nose started to bleed. When I got home, my dad tried to console me, telling me that balls-to-nose is just "one long muscle." I asked my dad, "If that's true, if I push on my nose, would it extend my penis, and would I be happier the rest of my life?"

I hate violence, but I also hate abuse, so if your kid could handle it, it'd be cool if he stood up for himself. I'd maybe get him tae kwon do lessons, if only that shit existed. In any case, please do not take this answer seriously, 'cause I don't know the real dynamic. But I'd love to see him stand up to those bullies and kick them all in the balls. I never said that, BTW. Turning the other cheek is good too, but a bully is a bully and sometimes a guy just needs to stand up for himself. It's tough to be caught between a cheek and balls. I believe it's called "the taint."

> My apologies for all of
> these answers.
> Bob

Allison Silverman

Dear Allison:
Is it appropriate to neck on a first date?
                          Jackie Kruller-Lerner
                          Huntington, NY

Dear Jackie:
What a quaint and delightful question! It is refreshing to hear from a youth like yourself with such old-fashioned values! "Necking" or "making out" can be daunting for inexperienced young people. Many fear that they will be labeled a "tease" if they "neck" a partner on the first date, but then refuse to take the next step and give him or her a "rimjob." In such cases, it can be helpful to remember the old saying: "First date we neck? Sure, what the heck! Then anilingus?

Not till next time you ring us!" As a reminder, I am sending you a sampler so you can cross-stitch this on a throw pillow. Good luck!

Allison

. . .

Dear Allison:

I am having trouble finding a job because I have a degree in English and everyone knows that is a fake degree. Should I do telemarketing or just let the earth have me?

Michelle
Portland, OR

Dear Michelle:

I would like to help you but, frankly, your letter is breathtakingly insensitive to those of us who majored in telemarketing. Are you under the impression that you can simply waltz into a telemarketing position without ever taking courses like "Introduction to Telemarketing: Conceptions of the Sensory," "Telemarketing Perspectives: The Poetics of American Humanism," or even "Gendered Identities: An Introduction to Black Queer Telemarketing"? And your equally cavalier approach to taking your own life—"let the earth have me"—betrays an utter ignorance of how much hard work and scholarship goes into suicide. Those blunders aside, I do have some good news. Your English degree makes you uniquely qualified to compose a poem belittling all the poor suckers who majored in philosophy. What a bunch of idiots!

Allison

...

Dear Allison:

I am a real estate broker who works in an office of roughly thirty people. I enjoy my job greatly, but one of my coworkers seems to dislike me. He has done things like put paint chips in my coffee mug, and he once replied-all to an office-wide e-mail with a message implying that I had been in jail for deviant sexual behavior. He said both incidents were accidents, but I am like 83 percent certain they weren't. How can I handle this situation without quitting my job?

Steve

St. Louis, MO

Dear Steve:

This is a serious matter. I strongly suggest you make an appointment as soon as possible with your human resources department. Bring a tape recorder to this and all following meetings. You will be asked to document every instance of your coworker's hostile behavior in a log. Then you will be told to show your log to the human resources manager. This is a crucial moment, Steve, and you will have to restrain yourself from acting out sexually. Though technically they

have ordered you to show them your "log," they are referring to your documentation of inappropriate work incidents
and not to your penis. Control yourself. Remember what
the guys in Cell Block D said they'd do to you if they ever
saw your face back in the pen. You can do this, Steve! If
it gets tough, do that old trick where you try to estimate
percentages to keep yourself from giving in to your sick,
deviant instincts.

Allison

. . .

Dear Allison:
Do I look slutty in this?

Diane Bullock
Brooklyn, NY

Dear Diane:
It breaks my heart when women question themselves about
looking or feeling sensual. We needn't be ashamed of our
sexuality. It is an essential part of our womanhood and of
that we should be proud! If I could wish anything for you,
Diane, it would be for you to spend less time worrying if
you look slutty and more time worrying if you look like a
tranny.

Allison

. . .

Dear Allison:
I'm really, really tired of answering the question "You ready for the weekend?" Who's ever not ready for the weekend? Any way to answer this without just saying, "Yes. I am ready for the weekend"?

> *Lorna Holden*
> *East Memphis, AR*

Dear Lorna:

The only way to get around this annoyance is to schedule some really ambitious weekends. Make arrangements to take toddlers camping. Volunteer to hunt an escaped felon. Plan to listen to six hours of your local public radio personality introducing the American Songbook. You will be woefully unprepared for the weekend, and when asked if you're ready for it, you will freak out and teach your questioner a lesson. Then renege on your vow to listen to public radio. You're not a martyr.

> Allison

...

Dear Allison:
What's one to do about the expanding snake population in the Florida Everglades? Friends or enemies?

> *Todd M.*
> *Jacksonville, FL*

Dear Todd:

You're from Jacksonville! I'm from Gainesville! I used to be on the debate team and we'd go up to Jax to compete against Terry Parker HS. Did you go to Terry Parker? I get so annoyed when I say I'm from the South and people are like, "No, you're not. You're from Florida." And I'm like, "I'm from North Florida. That's the South." They think all of Florida is Boca or Naples or something. And I always say that Tom Petty is from Gainesville and that Lynyrd Skynyrd and Molly Hatchet are from Jacksonville. And they're like, "Oh, I had no idea." Good thing you probably don't have to deal with that since you live down there and not in New York like I do now! Do you know that they call a cookout a "barbecue" up here? Like, they could be just grilling hamburgers but since they're doing it outside they call it a barbecue. I learned that the hard way (by going to a lot of so-called "barbecues"!). And when you tell people it's not a barbecue, they're like, "Oh, what do you know about barbecue? You're from Florida. That's not the South." And I'm like, "I'm from North Florida!" Anyway, thanks for your question about the Burmese pythons in the Everglades. It's pretty much a South Florida problem. So let those douchebags figure it out. Go Gators!

                                        Allison

. . .

Dear Allison:

When offering someone Tic Tacs, what is the appropriate number of individual mints to shake out of the container?

> *Holly F.*
>
> *Long Island, NY*

Dear Holly:

When I was a child, my mother would put two Tic Tacs in the front of her mouth and pretend she was a bunny rabbit. So, no more than one.

> Allison

...

Dear Allison:

My kid wants the latest thing. What is it?

> *Adrienne*

Dear Adrienne:

It's very hard to deliver up-to-the-minute information like the kind you request, Adrienne. The publication of a book can take a very long time. But because I believe there's some truly revolutionary technology on the horizon, I am willing to take the risk!

It's called a tea pouch.

You see, several months ago, a New York tea dealer named Thomas Sullivan was sending tea samples to prospective buyers. To catch the eyes of potential customers, he put his pinches of loose tea in little silk pouches. Well, the folks on the receiving end of these mailings had no idea the tea pouches were just for show. They didn't know what to do with them, so they tried dunking them in hot water. You will not believe what happened next. Exposed to the hot water that flowed through the pouch, the tea leaves brewed a perfect cup of tea. Yet the leaves themselves remained contained within the pouch and were easily discarded! You see, the tea leaves were trapped in the silk, but the water could flow freely around them. The leaves stayed in the pouch throughout the brewing!

Do you realize what this means, Adrienne? No more rinky-dink loose tea leaves in our tea. I'm really keen on this tea pouch! It's a humdinger!

I hope my exciting news is not out-of-date by the time this reaches you. As I said, the publication of a book can be a long process, and, until the canal is finished, we shall have to continue shipping our books on our old windjammer and pray each time that she survives one more trip around Cape Horn!

Allison

Nick Hornby

Dear Nick:

What, in your opinion, is the best song for lovemaking?
                                    Claire and Judd

Dear Claire and Judd:

There isn't one best song, of course. There are two. For common or garden-, post-TV sex, "Blitzkrieg Bop" by The Ramones is the one. It lasts a little over two minutes, and "Hey! Ho! Let's go" is a very useful opening chant, especially if you two have just started dating. The rhythm is good, too! If it's a scented-candle anniversary extravaganza, then you need Yes's prog-rock classic "Yours Is No Disgrace." My sexual partners have always appreciated the confidence-boosting title, which is helpfully repeated over and over in the chorus, and at over nine minutes, the song allows you to get through pretty much every sexual position ever invented, and still leaves you time for a smoke.

Nick

...

Dear Nick:

Can you please explain how the Amazon ranking system works?

David Carle

Estacada, OR

Dear David:

Say you have published a book. Well, if you look it up on Amazon, the ranking system will tell you how good it is, compared with all the other books that have ever been published. Glenn Beck's *The 7: Seven Wonders That Will Change Your Life,* for example, is, at the time of writing, the fifth greatest book ever written; Philip Roth's *American Pastoral,* by contrast, ranks at 15,441. (Mr. Roth should think about that, and learn from his mistakes, but that's not our concern here.) I say "at the time of writing" because people are writing great books every second of every day, so there is a chance that Glenn Beck will have slipped a bit by the time you read this. And a chance that Philip Roth will have climbed in the rankings. I doubt it, though.

I don't know you, David Carle, and I'm not going to do any research. But if you have written a book, I'm guessing that it's not as good as *The 7,* but it is better than *American*

Pastoral. This is true of a lot of books, more than fifteen thousand of them.

Nick

. . .

Dear Nick:
I make very little money and live below the nation's poverty line,
but I feel wealthy in my heart. Does this make me an idiot?

N. Lowen
Ann Arbor, MI

Dear N.:

You are either an idiot or you are pathologically lazy. One of the glories of the U.S.A., it seems to me, is that people who say things like, "I feel wealthy in my heart," and give every appearance of believing it, can simply write the sentiment down in a book and make a ton of money. (If they can't be bothered to write it down in a book, they can write it down in a movie script or in a song. The end result—an unstoppable flow of dollars—is the same.) You can't do that in Europe. Does "Heaven Knows I'm Miserable Now" sound like an American song title to you? That's how we make our money: by whining and complaining.

So the big question is, why haven't you written a book called *Wealthy In My Heart,* and become wealthy in your bank? Because you're idle and/or dumb—that's why. You have an added advantage: you come from a place that nobody has ever heard of, and where nobody wants to go. So if you really have achieved an inexplicable inner peace, people will totally buy into it.

Nick

...

Dear Nick:
Okay, let's put this matter to rest already! Who in the hell killed Kennedy?

Anonymous

Dear Anonymous:
I am from the UK, where we have our own problems, so it came as an awful shock to me to hear that President Kennedy had been killed—murdered, in fact, as I understand it. We are sorry for your loss, and stand shoulder-to-shoulder with you at this difficult time. Or we would have done this, if only we'd been paying more attention.

In an attempt to answer your question, however, I have done some Googling (which you could have done for yourself, to be honest). Anyway, the answer is that Carlos Marcello, Santo Trafficante, Jimmy Hoffa, Guy Banister, David Ferrie, Carlos Bringuier, Clay Shaw, Antoine Guerini, Lucien Sarti, Lyndon B. Johnson, J. Edgar Hoover, Clint Murchison Jr., Haroldson L. Hunt, E. Howard Hunt Jr. (no relation), Joachim Joesten, Bobby Baker, Jack Ruby, J. D. Tippit, Bernard Weissman, Nikita Khruschev, Frank

Sturgis, Johnny Roselli, Sam Giancana, Gerry Patrick Hemming, Lee Harvey Oswald, Edward Lansdale, Fidel Castro, George Hickey, Eladio del Valle, and Elvis Presley killed Kennedy. This seems bang on to me, although I am perplexed by the absence of women from this list. A couple of the women I know could assassinate a president without even feeling bad for a second. I'm pretty sure a woman would have been involved—probably Yvonne de Carlo, who played Lily Munster in the TV series made shortly after the assassination.

Nick

Weird Al Yankovic

Dear Weird Al:
My wife finally gave me permission to build my own "man cave"
in the basement. What are some essentials? I already have a beer
tap and a flat-screen TV, but what else should I have?
Tony Kastner
Gaithersburg, MD

Dear Tony:
You've already got an excellent start there. Just make sure
that the flat-screen measures at least as many inches diago-
nally as you are tall, minus the length of your forearm—
failing to meet that spec is a common mistake made by
first-time man cave builders.

Of course, you'll also want some of the essentials—a stack
of back issues of *Modern Bride,* a Ped Egg (with matching

Ped Egg caddie), a German-made antique gummi worm dispenser, a small albino alpaca (neutered), an inflatable wading pool filled with lavender and periwinkle Ping-Pong balls, a twelve-volt car battery with jumper cables, a box of sixty-four Crayola crayons (be sure to purchase the version with the built-in sharpener), a set of Hummel figurines (no dolphins!!!), and a Sparkletts water bottle filled with Astro-glide. Then I think you're all set.

> Good luck, and happy
> spelunking!
> Weird Al

. . .

Dear Weird Al:

At what age, in your opinion, is it most appropriate to lose your virginity? I'm seventeen and not in any rush, but am being pressured by my girlfriends.

> *Susan R.*

Dear Susan R.:

Don't let your slutty, whore-faced girlfriends pressure you into anything. Be your own person. But if you're asking for my advice (and apparently you are), I'd encourage you not to rush into it. I would definitely wait until you're married. In fact, just for good measure, I'd even wait a few years after that. I think perhaps the absolute best time to lose your vir-ginity is right after filling out the paperwork for the second mortgage on your home. That worked out just fine for me, and I'm sure it'll do the trick for you as well.

Weird Al

...

Dear Weird Al:
By what books have you been influenced the least? I'm only talking about the ones that had a really, really horrible and negative effect on you.

Raymond Jacobson
Los Angeles, CA

Dearest Raymond:
Hard to choose, but I'll narrow it down to two...

For sure, one would have to be the Los Angeles phone book (White Pages edition). Not only did it fill me with tremendous ennui, but it ultimately made me realize how small and unimportant I was in the overall scheme of things—how I was just one of many faceless, inconsequential life-forms in the greater Los Angeles area. And then when I got to the *Y*'s and realized that my own name wasn't even in there (I'm unlisted), it made me feel invisible—sort of like I didn't exist at all. I tell you, reading that book from cover to cover was one of the most soul-crushing experiences of my life.

The other book that has had a horrible, negative effect on me was *Beowulf* (the CliffsNotes edition), which I read in eighth grade. As soon as I found out that I could slide through class by skimming over a thin pamphlet, instead of torturing myself by reading a huge, ancient, stultifyingly boring book, I was on a slippery slope. Why make myself miserable putting in a lot of hard work when I could just take a quick, easy shortcut? It's this very philosophy that exacerbated my slow, horrifying descent into madness.

Weird Al

. . .

Dear Weird Al:
How can I tell my husband about the nose job I had before I met him?

Sarah
Brooklyn, NY

Dear Sarah:
Let me tell you, men love surprises. So here's what you do: Reproduce with him. And the second that poor, unfortunate baby with the grotesquely large, misshapen honker evacuates your birth canal, you can hold it out to your husband and shout, "Surprise! This is what my nose used to look like!" Then you'll both have a nice, long laugh.

Weird Al

. . .

Dear Weird Al:

I'm thinking of adopting a baby boy and naming him Braddock. My husband, on the other hand, claims this sounds like the name of a prison warden. I find his theory foolish. Can you settle this argument for us so we can get on with the adoption?

> *Dale Gregory*
> *Livonia, MI*

Dear Dale:

I'm afraid I'll have to side with your husband here, Dale. I've never met a guy named Braddock who hadn't spent a considerable chunk of his adult life confiscating shivs from hardened convicts. And more importantly, let me just say for the record, Braddock is a stupid, stupid name (no offense).

If I may be so bold as to suggest a more appropriate (i.e., less aggressively stupid) name for your child, I'd go with either Nathaniel or Superfly. Or, if it's a boy, Prometheus.

> Weird Al

The Parties Responsible

Judd Apatow wrote and directed the films *Knocked Up* and *Funny People* and was the cowriter and director of *The 40-Year-Old Virgin*. He was also the executive producer of the television series *Freaks and Geeks*.

Rob Baedeker is a member of the Kasper Hauser comedy group, author of *SkyMaul: Happy Crap You Can Buy from a Plane, Weddings of the Times*, and *Obama's BlackBerry*.

Anne Beatts has written for theater, film, television, radio, books, magazines, newspapers, and new media. She currently lives in Los Angeles with her seven-year-old daughter. If you want more, there's Google.

Elizabeth Beckwith's first book, *Raising the Perfect Child Through Guilt and Manipulation,* is in stores now.

Jerri Blank is the star of *Strangers with Candy,* a Comedy Central show and subsequent movie. She remains, as of this writing, fictional.

Roz Chast's cartoons have been published in such magazines as *The New Yorker, Scientific American,* the *Harvard Business Review, Redbook,* and *Mother Jones.* Her most recent book is a comprehensive compilation of her favorite cartoons called *Theories of Everything: Selected, Collected, and Health-Inspected Cartoons by Roz Chast, 1978–2006.* She also illustrated *The Alphabet from A to Y, with Bonus Letter, Z,* the bestselling children's book by Steve Martin.

Louis C.K. can be seen in the film *The Invention of Lying* and on the FX series *Lovie.* His Emmy-nominated special, *Louis C.K.: Chewed Up,* is available on CD and DVD.

Mike Doughty is a songwriter born in 1970. His album *Sad Man Happy Man* was released in 2009. His zip code is 11225.

Dave Eggers lives in California.

Rich Fulcher is best known for his roles in *The Mighty Boosh.* Most recently he has performed as his alter ego, Eleanor, playing sellout seasons in Australia and at the Edinburgh Fringe Festival. He's the author of *Tiny Acts of Rebellion,* and has also appeared in *Modern Problems in Science, Snuff Box,* and *Skins.*

Zach Galifianakis is an entertainer. He lives in several different locations in the United States. In a salad bar situation, this is how he would construct his salad: spinach, Bibb lettuce, radish, onion, brussels sprouts, shredded carrots, CUCUMBERS, croutons, garbanzo beans, peas, sunflower seeds, beets (but not too many), and ranch dressing with a touch of oil and vinegar.

Dan Guterman was the former head writer at *The Onion* and is currently a staff writer at *The Colbert Report*.

Nick Hornby is the author of the bestselling novels *Slam*, *A Long Way Down*, *How to Be Good*, *High Fidelity*, and *About a Boy*, and the memoir *Fever Pitch*.

Anthony Jeselnik was most recently a writer and performer on *Late Night with Jimmy Fallon*. His debut album, *Shakespeare*, was released on Comedy Central Records last fall.

Julie Klausner is a comedy writer and performer whose first book, *I Don't Care About Your Band*, was released in 2010. Her website, predictably, is julieklausner.com.

Lisa Lampanelli, comedy's "Queen of Mean," skyrocketed to comedy fame thanks to her showstopping performances on the Comedy Central roasts of Jeff Foxworthy, Pamela Anderson, Larry the Cable Guy, Flavor Flav, and Donald Trump. Her CD/DVD *Dirty Girl* was nominated for a Grammy for Best Comedy Album in 2007. She just released her autobiography, *Chocolate, Please: My Adventures in Food, Fat, and Freaks*.

Sam Lipsyte is a novelist and short story writer. His fiction and nonfiction have appeared in *Harper's*, *Esquire*, *GQ*, *Bookforum*, *The New York Times Book Review*, *The Paris Review*, and *Playboy*, among other places.

Liam Lynch is a writer/director/musician. He's created shows like MTV's *Sifl and Olly Show,* as well as movies such as *Sarah Silverman: Jesus Is Magic* and *Tenacious D: The Pick of Destiny.* Check out his free podcast, Lynchland, at liamlynch.net or on iTunes.

Merrill Markoe has authored numerous books of humorous essays and novels, including *It's My F---ing Birthday, What the Dogs Have Taught Me, Walking in Circles Before Lying Down, Nose Down, Eyes Up,* and, most recently, *Cool, Calm & Contentious.*

Rose McGowan was born in Italy and has starred in multiple iconic films and television series, including *Scream, Southie, Jawbreaker, The Black Dahlia, Death Proof, Planet Terror,* and *Charmed,* to name just a few. She will next be seen in the feature film *Conan.*

Miscellaneous Canadian Rock Musicians: Owen Pallett is from Toronto. Steve Bays is from Victoria. A. C. Newman is from Vancouver. Sara Quin is from Calgary. Steven Page is from Ontario. John Samson is from Winnipeg.

Laraine Newman is a writer/performer and a founding member of The Groundlings theater company. She's an original cast member of *Saturday Night Live.* Her film, television, animation, and writing credits can be found on her website, larainenewman. com. She lives in Los Angeles with her husband of twenty-one years and their two teenage daughters.

Patton Oswalt lives and drinks in Los Angeles.

The Pleasure Syndicate is a comedy group that has written, collectively and individually, for *The New Yorker, Esquire, The*

Onion, Conan O'Brien, *The Daily Show,* and *Vanity Fair,* as well as the book *SEX: Our Bodies, Our Junk.*

Bob Powers is the author of several humor books, including *Happy Cruelty Day!* and *You Are a Miserable Excuse for a Hero.* His long-running humor website is girlsarepretty.com.

Simon Rich is the author of two collections, *Free-Range Chickens* and *Ant Farm,* which was a finalist for the Thurber Prize for American Humor. He's written for *The New Yorker, Saturday Night Live,* and *Mad Magazine.* His first novel, *Elliot Allagash,* was published by Random House in 2010.

Bob Saget has starred in many successful television shows, but he's also been an out-of-his-mind stand-up comedian for over thirty years. From his HBO special to his scene-stealing cameos in *Entourage* and *The Aristocrats,* it's always effective as Saget embraces his dark side. For full tour dates visit bobsaget .com.

George Saunders has written for many publications, including *Harper's, The New Yorker, GQ,* and *McSweeney's.* He is the author of five books and story collections, including *CivilWarLand in Bad Decline, Pastoralia,* and *In Persuasion Nation,* which was a finalist for the Story Prize in 2007.

Kristen Schaal starred in the cult HBO hit *Flight of the Conchords,* and has appeared in movies like *Going the Distance, When in Rome,* and *Get Him to the Greek,* among many others. She coauthored a sex guide, *The Sexy Book of Sexy Sex,* with her boyfriend and *Daily Show* writer Rich Blomquist.

Paul Scheer cocreated *Human Giant* with Aziz Ansari, Rob Huebel, and Jason Woliner. He can currently be seen on the FX show *The League* and on Adult Swim in the upcoming *NTSF:SD:SUV*.

Amy Sedaris is the author of *I Like You: Hospitality Under the Influence* and *Simple Times: Crafts for Poor People*. She's also the president of the New York crafting club the Crafty Beavers.

Allison Silverman launched *The Colbert Report* as co–head writer and later helmed the show as executive producer. Her TV credits include *The Daily Show with Jon Stewart, Late Night with Conan O'Brien,* and *Portlandia*. Allison also writes for *The New Yorker* and is one half of the future comedy duo Silverman and TBD.

Paul Simms has written for *Late Show with David Letterman, The Larry Sanders Show,* and *NewsRadio,* which he also created. He currently writes for *The New Yorker,* among other publications.

Brendon Small is the writer, musician, and cocreator for Adult Swim's *Metalocalypse* and *Home Movies*. He is also the author of the highest-charting death metal album(s) in recorded history.

Jerry Stahl is the author of six books, including the narcotic memoir *Permanent Midnight* (made into a movie with Ben Stiller and Owen Wilson) and *I, Fatty* (optioned by Johnny Depp). His latest screenplay, *Hemingway & Gellhorn,* aired on HBO, in 2012.

Scott Thompson is a member of the famed sketch comedy troupe The Kids in the Hall. One of his most famous characters is featured in a graphic novel, *Danny Husk: Hollow Planet,* released last year by IDW.

Fred Willard is an American comedian, actor, and voice-over actor known for his improvisational comedy skills. He is also known for his roles in the films *This Is Spinal Tap, Waiting for Guffman, Best in Show, A Mighty Wind,* and *For Your Consideration.*

Cintra Wilson is a culture critic and author whose books include *A Massive Swelling: Celebrity Re-Examined as a Grotesque, Crippling Disease, Caligula for President: Better American Living Through Tyranny,* and the novel *Colors Insulting to Nature.* She is currently writing the Critical Shopper column for *The New York Times* and working on her fourth book, *Fear and Clothing: Unbuckling America's Fashion Destiny.*

"Weird Al" Yankovic is a three-time Grammy winner and a sixth-grade spelling bee winner. His first children's book, *When I Grow Up,* was recently released by HarperCollins.

Alan Zweibel, an original *Saturday Night Live* writer, is currently finishing a new play titled *Sunday Nights at 8:00* to be directed by Jerry Zaks; he's also producing a documentary on the history of comedy with Steve Carell and David Steinberg, and writing a novel with Dave Barry.

YOU'RE A HORRIBLE PERSON, BUT I LIKE YOU
The Believer *Book of Advice*

The Believer magazine presents a compendium of advice from producers, writers, and actors of *The Office*, *Saturday Night Live*, *The Simpsons*, *Knocked Up*, *Flight of the Conchords*, *The Daily Show*, *Arrested Development*, *Reno 911!*, and *The Hangover* along with other people who should really never give advice. In these pages Fred Armisen offers help telling your dad you're a lesbian—give him the phone number and he'll do it for you. Mindy Kaling provides guidance on ending things with your mistress—dude, you totally have to kill her. Rainn Wilson offers insight on contacting that girl you dreamed about last night—he has created an all-purpose web portal for such interactions. Amy Sedaris identifies the best way to a man's heart—bone saw through the chest cavity.

Humor